FAREWELL TO
MATTERS OF PRINCIPLE

ODÉON

JOSUÉ V. HARARI AND VINCENT DESCOMBES
General Editors

HERMENEUTICS AS POLITICS
Stanley Rosen

FAREWELL TO MATTERS OF PRINCIPLE
Philosophical Studies
Odo Marquard

Farewell to Matters of Principle

Philosophical Studies

ODO MARQUARD

Translated by Robert M. Wallace
with the assistance of
Susan Bernstein and James I. Porter

New York   Oxford
OXFORD UNIVERSITY PRESS
1989

Oxford University Press

Oxford   New York   Toronto
Delhi   Bombay   Calcutta   Madras   Karachi
Petaling Jaya   Singapore   Hong Kong   Tokyo
Nairobi   Dar es Salaam   Cape Town
Melbourne   Auckland

and associated companies in
Berlin   Ibadan

Library of Congress Cataloging-in-Publication Data
Marquard, Odo.
Farewell to matters of principle: philosophical studies
Odo Marquard.
p.   cm. — (Odéon)
ISBN 0-19-505114-9   1. Philosophy.   I. Title.
B29.M36774   1989   100—dc20   89-32850   CIP

2 4 6 8 9 7 5 3 1

Printed in the United States of America
on acid-free paper

Contents

FAREWELL TO
MATTERS OF PRINCIPLE

= 1 =

Farewell to Matters of Principle
(Another Autobiographical Introduction)[a]

Philosophy, writes Aristotle, is the "science that investigates the first principles and causes."[1] It seeks principles, and pushing principiality even further, the ultimate principle among principles.

In that case, does "farewell to matters of principle" mean "farewell to philosophy"? This question is identical with the question, whether skeptics do or do not properly count as philosophers; for, far from proclaiming an adherence to critical rationalism (the dogmatism of whose antidogmatism I find disturbing),[b] the wording of the title to this little volume is meant to affirm the *skeptical* turn. This turn to skepticism in philosophy has been my path, and my task, up to the present. And so, to report on this—in a partially autobiographical manner, but with limited recourse to narrative—would seem an appropriate undertaking for an introduction to a collection of essays that document some of the more recent stages of my progress on this path. This report will fall into three parts: (1) the skeptical generation; (2) deferred disobedience; and (3) skepticism and finitude.

Notes added by the translator are marked with superior letters.

The Skeptical Generation

Skepticism is an old affair. So of course it is part of the history of philosophy, which has witnessed the Pyrrhonian and Academic skepticisms of the Hellenistic period; the moralistic skepticism of Montaigne and Charron; the Enlightenment skepticism of Bayle and Hume; the anthropological skepticism of Schulze's *Aenesidemus* and of Plessner; the historical skepticism of Burckhardt; and the antihistorical skepticism of Löwith. Skepticism is thus a clearly identifiable tradition of philosophy, and a long-standing one. How does it happen that someone from my generation, in particular, got involved in this (and without having known, initially, that such a coherent tradition existed)?

Helmut Schelsky, in his book *Die skeptische Generation* [The skeptical generation], which first appeared in 1957,[2] attempted an answer to this question. The turn to skepticism in Germany, according to Schelsky, was not the exception but the rule for the generation to which I, born in 1928, belong: namely, those who were no longer children and not yet adults (cf. pp. 16ff.) in, at least, the early part of the period between 1945 and 1955 (cf. pp. 5ff.). Schelsky demarcates the following "historical phases" and "generational types" of juvenile behavior since the turn of the century; "(1) the generation of the *Jugendbewegung* (youth movement); (2) the generation of political youth; (3) German youth in the decade following World War II, for whom we have provisionally chosen the label, 'the skeptical generation'" (p. 57). There was, then, the pre-Green generation of the Meissner formula,[c] of hiking, guitars, and recorders. Then came, between the wars, the generation of radical political and ideological engagement on behalf of a better world. Finally, after World War II, they were followed by the skeptical generation. Its skepticism—and Schelsky's interpretation certainly agrees with mine here—was a response to the "generation of political youth," and to the debacles in which that generation became involved and which they brought after them; a response, in other words, to the manner in which they had compromised themselves, which was perceived in two ways: in the experience of the older members (a contested, and certainly a contestable judgment), that the left failed;[3] and, in the experience of the younger members as well (in the face of horrible evidence, a judgment that is incontestable), that the right ushered in catastrophe. The shock of disillusionment had as its consequence, "in the consciousness of youth, a process of depoliticization, and a withdrawal from ideology" (p. 84). Thus this generation became "more critical, skeptical, and distrustful, more disbelieving, or at the very least more disillusioned than any generation of youth before it" (p. 488). "This sobered mentality made possible what, for the young, has been an unusual competence in dealing with life. In its private and social behavior, this generation is better adjusted, more realistic and capable of initiative, and surer of success than the youth of any previous period" (ibid.). With its "sharpened sense of reality," of what is "practical and reliable" (p.88)—with its "faith in what is concrete" (pp. 89, 307–8), and its "precocious maturity" (p. 93)—it became "the German edition of the generation that consolidated industrial society in general" (p. 493). Insofar as this generation really was skeptical, I shared in its fate—through my turn to skepticism.

For, to repeat, the skeptical turn was for the generation to which I belong not the exception but the rule. The only exceptional thing, in my case, was that with this turn to skepticism I landed among the philosophers, and then remained with them, as well. For as a rule the choice of philosophy as a field of study meant, then as it does now, not the beginning of a successful career, but the beginning of a personal tragedy; and in any event, it does not signify "faith in the concrete." As a student of philosophy, and one who also studied German literature, as well as art history, then history, and finally evangelical theology and a little Catholic fundamental theology, I certainly did not find myself on the same path as those "cautious, but successful young men" (p. 488) with their "sharpened sense of reality" and of "the practical and reliable" (p. 88)—no, by Zeus, certainly not there! One concomitant factor in this embargo against the "concrete," which I seem to have launched, may well have been the years 1940–1945, which I spent, until immediately after my seventeenth birthday, at a political boarding school,[4] a late and extreme socializing agency of the "generation of political youth." Solidly trained only in ignorance of the world (after the conclusion of the war and a brief stint as a prisoner of war), I was a latecomer to the historical reality that was shared by the skeptical generation; and, further delayed by the student's reprieve from everyday economic necessity, I managed to learn only half of that generation's lessons: to wit, not the "concrete" competence in dealing with reality, but *only* the skepticism. It was just that, of course, that led me to philosophy, and did so by way of a substitute enthusiasm for art—for the attempt to make reality more attractive, by means of tones, images, and words, as an enticement to remaining alive—and for art's seductions, which are seductions precisely not to self-realization, but to self-"possibilization." I traveled, in other words, by way of esthetics.

Thus, after the modest coincidence that I was admitted, during the 1947 period of *numerus clausus* (restricted admission), not to the programs in Marburg or Kiel, but to Münster, it was hardly a coincidence that I immediately came across, there, the philosopher who would later become my mentor: Joachim Ritter. For at that time he was beginning to give his lectures on "philosophical esthetics," which, being a theory of esthetics as compensation, both described and criticized the "position of possibility," and thereby spoke directly to my concerns.[5, d] It was moreover through this same course of lectures that, even before his later lectures on practical philosophy in which he formulated his approach positively, Ritter won over the older elements of that diverse and controversial farrago of pupils who would later play a significant role, in the history of West German philosophical institutions, as the wing of hermeneutical thought that would rehabilitate practical philosophy. The liveliness of the Ritter school was a result not only of the talents of individuals but also of the "heterogeneous composition of Ritter's 'Collegium Philosophicum'; which combines Thomists, evangelical theologians, positivists, logicians, Marxists, and skeptics."[6] For Ritter did not bind his pupils to his own positions.[7]

From Ritter I learned—apart from those positions—that noticing is more important than deduction; that no one can start from the very beginning, and that everyone must link up with what has gone before (in other words, a sense of history); that contradictions ought, if necessary, to be borne, and their apparent solution resisted; that such contradictions are more powerfully present in persons than on paper; that this demands that one encounter alien attitudes firsthand and be able to learn from them; and that, accordingly, the more diverse the constellation of philosophers the better. I also learned to appreciate institutions and the obligations that go with them; and finally, I learned that experience—the experience of life—is indispensable for philosophy. Experience without philosophy is blind; philosophy without experience is empty: one cannot really have a philosophy without first having the experience to which it is the answer. But experience takes time. Thus, Ritter's pupils converged, in their substantive positions, neither in the course of their studies nor in their years of apprenticeship, but only decades afterward: when they had accumulated experiences of their own, in the light of which Ritter's own philosophical answers could now seem plausible. There exists in the Ritter school—I can detect it today—a convergence around a common ground, which was a long-term, delayed effect. At that time, however, when we were students, there were no limits—apart, that is, from institutional obligations, and the evident concern that Ritter felt for each of us—to our freedom of thought, including the freedom to be a skeptic.

In 1958 I sought to formulate the concept of "skepticism in the interim" as a "position, in the nautical sense," in my book *Skeptische Methode im Blick auf Kant* [Skeptical method in view of Kant]. It was a published version, almost entirely rewritten, of the dissertation for which I received my degree in 1954 at Freiburg, under the generous encouragement of my director, Max Müller[8] (Ritter had gone off to Istanbul for three years). The book was considered, stylistically, a highly individual document. As a substitute for time pressure, under conditions of leisure, form is one way to eliminate gratuitousness, and thus deserves to be counted among the norms of production for those to whom writing does not come easily. It is normal, in a curriculum vitae, for much that is important to fail to enter into the account: the intimate aspects, the difficulties (there is, you know, a fundamental right to ineffability). I feel, and I began to feel then, that one should seek ongoing dealings, in philosophy, only with such ideas as one also thinks of during the difficult situations in life, and which, if need be, one can live with one's whole life long. That does not exclude, as I learned chiefly from Kierkegaard and Heine, the search for light and pointed formulation. Far from being the opposite of seriousness, esthetic play in composition and formulation are an external form that it takes: the form that takes seriousness so seriously that it finds it necessary to make seriousness more bearable. And that is how I arrived at my genre: transcendental belles lettres.

Deferred Disobedience

The intellectual climate of the Bundesrepublik changed: the "skeptical generation" was followed by a new "generation of political youth." In philosophy, it was preceded by the success of the Frankfurt School among those who now no longer counted as "youth." I too was deeply impressed by the Critical Theory of Horkheimer and Adorno. In 1956 I presented an affirmative and promotional paper on Herbert Marcuse's *Eros and Civilization*[9] to the reading circle of the Collegium Philosophicum. At the time I was already at work on my inaugural dissertation on Schelling and Freud,[10] the argument of which was that psychoanalysis, viewed philosophically, is the continuation of German Idealism by disenchanted means.

Particularly in *Totem and Taboo*,[11] in his theory of conscience, Freud made use of a concept of "deferred obedience" (pp. 143ff.): the sons, in the "primal horde," having murdered their father, "revoked their deed by forbidding the killing of the totem, the substitute for their father; and they renounced its fruits by resigning their claim to the women who had now been set free" (p. 143). "Totem religion," like the conscience, which followed it, "arose from the filial sense of guilt, in an attempt to allay that feeling and to appease the father by deferred obedience to him" (p. 145). The successful rebellion against the father was replaced, after the fact, by respect for what took the place of the father. In the Bundesrepublik, I believe, precisely the opposite phenomenon occurred, beginning at the end of the 1950s, and continuing in the spectacular reprise that was the "student movement" at the end of the 1960s. The revolt against the dictator (the father of the "fatherless society"[12]), which largely failed to take place between 1933 and 1945, was symbolically made up for in the rebellion against what had taken the place of the dictatorship after 1945. This is why precisely the "totems" now were slaughtered and eaten, and the "taboos" broken. After the material phase of gorging came the ideological one. There arose a free-floating, quasi-moral need for revolt, a need that was just looking for opportunities for discharge. In accordance with the logic of "deferment," this need directed itself, opportunistically and indiscriminately, against what happened to be there at the time: against the conditions of the Bundesrepublik—that is, conditions that were democratic, liberal, and eminently worth preserving. To jeopardize these for the sake of a revolutionary principle was—and here I will be quite blunt ("one is never less patient than with errors from which one has just freed oneself": Goethe)—simply stupidity celebrated as "reflection." For there are no guarantees against changing things for the worse, not even—and especially not—by means of the revolutionary philosophy of history, which thinks that the idea of progress provides such a guarantee.[13] We have—all of us have, in our day and our part of the world—much more to lose than just our chains.[14] All of this was ignored by the deferred protest, by which a democracy became the deferred object of the indignation of a rebellion that had not taken place against a totalitarian dictatorship. Such is the absurdity that is involved in the peculiar deferred character of this protest. The opposite of Freud's concept of "deferred obedience" suggests itself as an apt description of this phenomenon. So I will call what took place here between the late 1950s and the early 1970s "deferred disobedience."

It was the age of reversed totemism, which has its own peculiar mechanisms and reactions. To take just a few examples: totemism leads to demonstrative asceticism; reversed totemism leads to demonstrative libertinism, which understands itself as an emancipatory and antiauthoritarian movement. In totemism, on Freud's interpretation, the rebellion against a human being (the father) leads to a compulsive and deferred worship of animals (the totem); in reversed totemism, the rebellion that did not take place against the political beast, the "Leviathan," leads to a belated rebellion against real fathers and real human beings. There may sometimes be a significant correlation—whether the analysis is in terms of individuals or in terms of groups—between the intensity of former conformity and the intensity of present radicalism. The fact that an action was omitted also now (belatedly) forces every thought to proceed immediately to action—disregarding Spinoza's insight that one may think whatever one pleases only so long as one does not also do whatever one pleases.[15]

But above all there is the compulsion to find a secondary resemblance between then and now: because fascism was the target against which a revolt did not materialize then, today the target of the compensatory revolt must also be fascism, and is stylized as such by means of an appropriate array of theories. For otherwise the quantity of absurdity in the (only deferred) disobedience would be all too flagrant, and it would be all too clear that the present form of disobedience is, as a rule, a comfortable one that does not cost the disobedient person very much. This is why the negative characterization of present things by identifying them with past things—the technique of detecting a hair in every soup, alienation in every reality, repression in every institution, power and fascism in every relationship—becomes a highly developed art. If necessary, an additional negativity can be applied by "making the good evil"[16] and "borrowing misery."[17] Differences between then and now that simply cannot be interpreted away are regarded as added villainies on the part of the present—as especially infamous camouflage—so that differences themselves become proofs of similarity. No one seems to realize that this secondary discovery of similarity between the present and the past would practically be predestined to make fascism seem harmless, if anyone really were to believe in it—a possibility that evidently is never seriously reckoned with.

The deferred disobedience did not occur immediately after the end of World War II, but later, and this was not by chance. "Erst kommt das Fressen, dann kommt die Moral" (first fill your belly, then worry about ethics) (Brecht). Only once conditions were made materially tolerable, through the postwar reconstruction, and then brought to a level of surplus, did dismay with the horrors of the past fully reach the conscience of Germany, and only then, as it were by time-delay, did it become morally really intolerable. Only then did one find time for feelings of guilt, for discontent with one's own historical past. This is why it was only then, too, and never earlier, that the opportunity for disencumbering oneself that was present by the unmasking critique of alienation became largely irresistable, and popular. This critique was quickly monopolized by the revolutionary philosophy of history into which Critical Theory—despite the immediate opposition of its original inventors and advocates—had been further developed.

The key to this disencumbering process is the realization that one no longer needs to *have* a conscience—when it is overburdened by reproaches of guilt—if one can *be* the conscience. Deferred obedience gives rise to the kind of conscience that one *has,* but deferred *dis*obedience gives rise to the kind of conscience that one *is:* the tribunal that one evades by becoming it. The recipe for success that was exploited by the critique practiced by the adherents of the revolutionary philosophy of history was to convert this flight from having a conscience to being the conscience into the principle of the avant-garde, and to use it as the foundation for their claim that it was only the others who represented the past, while they themselves represented only the future—by virtue, precisely, of the deferred refusal that I have been discussing. One of Brecht's *Stories of Mr. Keuner* bears the title, "Measures Taken against Violence."[18] It relates the story of a certain Mr. Egge, who during the period of violence knew how to accommodate himself, moderately, to circumstances, and who said No only after the period of violence was past. This story—as I suggested later in my contribution to the sixth colloquium (1972) of the group Poetics and Hermeneutics,[19] of which I have been a member since 1966 (and whose driving mechanism was and is Hans Robert Jauss)—is relevant to what I have been discussing here: it is a fragment of a parable of deferred disobedience.

All of this belongs in an autobiographical introduction because it is based in part on introspection: on an analysis of my own participation in the Movement, during the 1960s, and of my reversal of sympathies and my cancelation of that participation—my refusal to refuse. I suppose that this refusal of mine (it set in only in 1967: I am a slow learner, and have a long braking distance) was made easier by the fact that I had now made up for the neglect of the concrete, which had accompanied my previous "pure" skepticism.

For in the meantime I had taken the step from "preexistence" to "existence,"[20] by marrying (1960) and becoming a father, instead of persisting, as an artist in unmasking, in a permanent process of reflection; and I had finally satisfied the institutional requirements for an academic career (1963) and taken on the professional duties of a university teacher. I became an assistant professor in Münster, and in 1965 a department chairman and full (after the higher education reform, no longer quite so "full") professor in Giessen. Eventually I was made a dean, and since then, inevitably, I have played—and have not evaded—a number of roles in academic administration and in educational and university politics. What Gide's Armand says about his family in *The Counterfeiters*—"We live off of papa's faith"—holds good, in modified form, for my own family: they have lived off of papa's doubts and despair, and his talent for mixing this working capital with an appropriate quantity of erudition and for converting it into didactic and transcendental-belletristic formulations. And in the long run—beginning with my second job—the life they have led has not been all that bad. They would have been able to lead a far better life if I had also expanded and rounded out this working capital of mine with an assortment of revolutionary sentiments, and theories to match.

Then, however, a certain level of discord would have been surpassed, in my case as it was in others, by the contradictions characteristic of the whole period: that is, by the divergence and increasing unrelatedness of the world of reflection and the life-world, the world of expectation and the world of experience, the world of sentiments and the world of responsibilities, the world of reform and the world of work, the world of intention and the world of action, the world of indignant rebellion and the world that one can believe in.

Skepticism and Finitude

The long-term intolerability of this discrepancy, I believe, led to what has been called the *Tendenzwende* ["tendential turning-point"].[c] It was an injection of honesty into circumstances that needed it. For immediate concerns as against ultimate ones have rights, too.

This new sobriety went hand in hand with regrets in regard to the (now manifest) illusory content of deferred disobedience. I at least was vexed by the fact that skepticism itself had led me into a new blind faith. There would appear—disconcertingly—to be something like a conservation law for naivety: the human capacity for mistrust is limited, and the more it is concentrated on one mental "front," the easier it is for naivety to gain the upper hand on other fronts. The contemporary scene is agitated by aggressive measures against this disconcerting experience. Thus our poets, for example, have turned into seething souls: almost all of them seethe, either with rage or on the stove (or both), and that always produces books. I myself am unable to seethe, except, perhaps, with mere water; but even that—*tristesse oblige!*— yielded a book: *Schwierigkeiten mit der Geschichtsphilosophie* [Difficulties with the philosophy of history] (1973), which sought to draw up an interim balance sheet.

Philosophy, be it the philosophy of deferred disobedience or the rampant doubts of mere skepticism, is not an amulet that protects its bearer against straying down the wrong paths. I resented this and laid the blame on philosophy. The result of this disappointment was the essay, "Competence in Compensating for Incompetence?," written in 1973 for the sixtieth birthday of Hermann Krings and reprinted as the second essay in this collection. Of course, in this piece my skepticism toward philosophy goes too far; but just this makes it another representative example of the specifically German "uncertainty of philosophy about itself,"[21] and the ensuing despair, which is the (historically conditioned) flip side of an exaggerated hope that was placed in philosophy. For the "belated nation," as Plessner has shown, initially compensates for its deficit in liberal political realities (which is a consequence of the nation's belatedness) by pinning excessive hopes on intellectualism, and especially on philosophy. And yet philosophy can only dash this misplaced hope: witness its trajectory through the nineteenth century, in the course of which, for just that reason, the fine art of hope-dashing arose—the critique of ideology. Unlike, for example, the Anglo-Saxon democracies, whose demands on philosophy could be of a more modest character from the start, in Germany this development only produced an inclination to exchange absolute hopes pinned on philosophy for an absolute despair over philosophy. My essay on philosophy's "competence in compensating for incompetence" was of the same mold. But at bottom the hope expressed there was to see philosophy abandon its presumptuousness.[22] And in this sense the essay marks a reiteration and an affirmation of the skeptical turn.

However, this skeptical turn, repeated and reaffirmed, had to become more skeptical with respect to itself, particularly as the disquieting suspicion began to well up that it was indirectly encouraging illusions about the potential for making a better world. The only choice at this point was to reduce its capacity for illusion, by taking the portion of quasi-divine sovereignty, which permanent doubt seems to involve, and linking it inseparably to humanity, and by redefining skepticism (by, if you like, accenting its "existential" aspect) into a *philosophy of finitude*.

With this shift, doubt was now balanced by other features that skepticism (as the historical record shows) had always also had: taking the "individual" seriously, and being willing to live in accordance with "ancestral customs"—that is, to do what is "usual"—as long as there is no compelling reason to deviate from that. Such observance is inevitable for human beings, because they are individuals. It is true that what skepticism would like to have is "avoidable" individuality: cultivated individuality. But what it counts on in fact is unavoidable individuality, which all human beings have because they must die their own death, and because they exist "toward death."[23] Life is always too brief to allow one to disengage oneself as much as one would like from what one already is, by changing oneself. One simply does not have time for that. So one must always remain, for the most part, what one already, historically, was: one must "link up."

A future needs a derivation: "The choice that I am"[24] is supported by the nonchoice that I am; and the latter is always so much the greater part, for us, that it also (on account of the shortness of our lives) surpasses our ability to provide it with a rational grounding. Thus if, given the lack of time that goes with our *vita brevis*, we want to engage in rational grounding at all, we must provide grounds not for our nonchoices, but for our choices, for the things we change. The burden of proof is on the one who proposes changes.

When skepticism adopts this rule,[25] which flows from human mortality, it tends toward the conservative. "Conservative" here is to be understood as an entirely unemphatic concept, the meaning of which is best exemplified by surgeons when they are debating whether they can proceed conservatively, or whether they have to remove the kidney, tooth, arm, or intestine. The rule of the art is that one cuts only if one has to (only if there are compelling reasons), otherwise not, and one never cuts everything. There is no such thing as an operation that does not involve a conservative procedure: one cannot lop off the entire person, given a single person. Intentionally or not, this is what those who shun the concept of "conservatism" overlook. Analogously, not everything can be changed, and consequently not every failure to change can be indicted. Thus those who, from the philosophers of history to the philosophers of "discourse," do just this by "overtribunalizing reality," produce something different from what they intend. This is what I wanted to show, by examining the initial constellation of this relationship, in the essay (written in 1978), "Indicted and Unburdened Man in Eighteenth-Century Philosophy," which is reprinted as the third essay in this volume: overtribunalizers establish not absolute rationality, but an "escape into untriability," which espouses freedoms that we (prior to all principled permission) already are; among them being our "usual" modes of behavior. Because death comes too soon to permit total changes and total rational groundings, we need these "usages," including the usage that philosophy is.

Skeptics deal, in other words, with the inevitability (due to our mortality) of traditions; and what is known—usually, and with the status of the usual[26]—in those domains, they know too. Thus skeptics are not those who as a matter of principle know nothing; it is just that they do not know anything that is a matter of principle. Skepticism is not the apotheosis of perplexity; it is simply a bidding *farewell to matters of principle.*

By contrast, the aim of the philosophy of principles is precisely to know matters of principle, in a principled way; this is why it seeks principles, and the ultimate principle among principles. This absolute principle, however, which (however it may be conceived) always *is,* as it were, the conscience that reality is supposed to *have,* transforms factual reality in its entirety into that which no longer can be taken for granted—into the contingent, the unjustified—which must first of all be redeemed from this unprincipled or even antiprincipled state by a principled justification: by a grounding in principles, or a change based on principles. As such a "metamorphosis" of reality into a thing that needs justification—as, in its tendency, a tribunalization of reality—the philosophy of principles is a key instance of change. If, however, it is true—as a fact conditioned by our mortality—that the burden of proof lies with one who proposes change, then it follows that, if de facto reality is, precisely because of its transitory character, the a priori behind all principles, what the philosophy of principles has to justify first is not de facto reality but itself.[27]

But both of the justifications that are involved in the philosophy of principles—the justification of principles in the face of the real, and the justification of the real in the face of principles—arrive either empty-handed or too late: that is, as an infinite answer addressed to a finite creature, always only after his death. If the transcendental hare really were (improbably) to arrive on the run, bearing tidings of matters of principle, and if his news were really about something, and not nothing, the finite tortoise would always already be found lying there: dead. Principles are long, life is short. We cannot spend our lives waiting for principled permission finally to begin living, because our death comes more quickly than the principles do—which is why we are forced to bid them farewell. This is why the finite human creature—with a provisional ethics for the time being, which is to say, in any case, until its death—must live without principled justification (so that conscience is always more a solitary than a universal thing, and maturity is above all the capacity for solitariness). This finite being must be contingent, and base its life on contingencies. But for this being, whose task it is to link up—and who does not stand before these contingencies like Buridan's ass before the piles of hay, but rather is involved in them, and can never extract himself from them more than a little—they are not arbitrary facts from which he can pick and choose arbitrarily, but rather (as the nonchoice that he is) they are fates over which he has no power of disposition and from which he can scarcely escape. For this reason—and this is the thesis of the essay, "The End of Fate? Some Observations on the Inevitability of Things

Over Which We Have No Power of Disposition" (1976), which is reprinted as the fourth item in this volume—while it is true that fate was displaced, theologically and metaphysically, by the absolute principle of the One God, this displaced fate promptly returned—at the latest, after the "end of God," which gave rise to modernity—in the form of our lack of disposition over what is pregiven, and our lack of disposition over the consequences. To depend on contingencies—that is, to have a fate—is unavoidable for human beings, on account of their mortality.

All these considerations spell farewell to a principled philosophy, but not to that unprincipled philosophy, skepticism. They spell farewell, for human beings, to principled freedom, but not to real freedom, which consists in freedoms, in the plural. These come about as a result of the motleyness of what is pregiven: as a result of the fact that the plurality—the rivalry, the counterbalancing opposition, the balance—of its powers either neutralizes or limits their grip on the individual. Freedoms are the result of the separation of powers. An appreciation of these freedoms is found not in the philosophy of principles, but in skepticism. This appreciation affects, at the same time, the role played by skeptical doubt; as the separation even of those powers that we call our convictions, *skeptical doubt is an appreciation of the separation of powers.* Skepticism's doubt is not absolute perplexity, but is rather a manifold sense of the *isosthenes diaphonia* (evenly balanced disagreement),[28] the balance, not only of conflicting dogmas, but also of conflicting realities—which by that very fact (*divide et liberaliter vive!*) allows individuals freedoms and vouchsafes them the relief from the absolute that is also and above all provided, as Hans Blumenberg has shown,[29] by the separation of powers in myth.

I asserted this (following very much in the footsteps of Blumenberg[30]) in an essay written early in 1978 and reprinted as the fifth essay of this volume: "In Praise of Polytheism. On Monomythic and Polymythic Thinking." Freedom does not consist in being allowed, "monomythically," to have only a single history, but rather in, "polymythically," having many of them, by separating even the powers that stories are. In case of necessity, one must promote this motleyness and multiplicity; and that is at least one of the functions of hermeneutics.

In the sixth and last essay in this volume—"The Question, To What Question Is Hermeneutics the Answer?" (1979)—I sought to under-score (by way of a late, long overdue affirmation of my membership in the hermeneutical camp) the fact that hermeneutics is the art, which is vitally important for human beings, of orienting oneself by means of "understanding"[f] among contingencies that one has both to hold fast to and to distance from oneself, because it is possible to get free of them only to a limited degree, given a limited lifespan. The most typically modern aspect of this vital art consists (under the motto, "read and let read!") in taming the "Absolute Text"—which had be-come the deadly point of contention in the hermeneutical civil wars (the wars of religion)—by reducing it to a "relative text," to a neutral, literary, esthetic text among other relative texts, by pluralizing read-ings and receptions, as well. This represents a separation of the powers that texts and interpretations are, so that it is now possible to say that "the core of hermeneutics is skepticism, and the important form of skepticism today is hermeneutics." We must bear with our contin-gency: skepticism, in particular—including the version of it that was laid out in the foregoing introduction—is not an absolute pronounce-ment, because every philosophy remains entangled in a life that is always too difficult and too brief to allow it to reach absolute clarity about itself. "Life," the saying goes, "is difficult, but it is good prac-tice." Above all, it trains us, *more sceptico,* to acquiesce, in various ways, in the fact that it is, after all, finite.

Notes

1. Aristotle, *Metaphysics,* A2 982b7ff., trans. W. D. Ross in *The Basic Works of Aristotle,* R. McKeon, ed. (New York, 1941), p. 692.
2. H. Schelsky, *Die skeptische Generation. Eine Soziologie der deutschen Jugend* (Düsseldorf/Cologne, 1957). I cite the fourth printing (1960).
3. Cf. M. Sperber, *Die vergebliche Warnung* (Vienna, 1973), pp. 165ff.
4. Cf. H. Scholz, *Nationalsozialistische Ausleseschulen. Internatsschulen als Herr-schaftsmittel des Führerstaats* (Göttingen, 1973), esp. pp. 162ff. (on the "Vorgeschichte und Entwicklung der Adolf-Hitler-Schulen 1936–1941"), pp. 254ff., 374ff.
5. On esthetics as compensation, see O. Marquard, "Kunst als Kompensation

ihres Endes," in W. Oelmüller, ed., *Ästhetische Erfahrung*, Kolloquium: Kunst und Philosophie, vol. 1 (Paderborn, 1981), pp. 159–68.

6. R. Spaemann, "Philosophie zwischen Metaphysik und Geschichte," *Neue Zeitschrift für systematische Theologie*, 1 (1959) 313; cf. H. Lübbe et al., eds., *Collegium Philosophicum. Studien, Joachim Ritter zum 60. Geburtstag* (Basel/ Stuttgart, 1965).

7. Summed up in J. Ritter, *Metaphysik und Politik. Studien zu Aristoteles und Hegel* (Frankfurt, 1969), and idem, *Subjektivität* (Frankfurt, 1974).

8. Cf. H. Müller, *Symbolos* (Munich, 1967), p. 49.

9. H. Marcuse, *Eros and Civilization. A Philosophical Inquiry into Freud* (Boston, 1955), and *Triebstruktur und Gesellschaft* (Frankfurt, 1965).

10. O. Marquard, "Über die Depotenzierung der Transzendentalphilosophie. Einige philosophische Motive eines neueren Psychologismus in der Philosophie," Habilitationsschrift, Münster, 1963, published as *Transzendentaler Idealismus, romantische Naturphilosophie, Psychoanalyse* (Cologne: Dinter, 1987).

11. S. Freud, *Totem and Taboo* (1912). Page references are to J. Strachey's translation in *Complete Psychological Works*, vol. 13 (London, 1955).

12. Cf. A. Mitscherlich, *Auf dem Weg zur vaterlosen Gesellschaft. Ideen zur Sozialpsychologie* (Munich, 1968).

13. Cf. R. Koselleck, *Kritik und Krise. Ein Beitrag zur Pathogenese der bürgerlichen Welt* (Freiburg/Munich, 1959).

14. Cf. M. Merleau-Ponty, *Die Abenteuer der Dialektik* (1955; Frankfurt, 1968), esp. pp. 245ff.

15. Cf. Spinoza, *Tractatus theologico-politicus* (1670), esp. pp. 301ff., in the German translation of G. Gawlick, *Theologisch-politischer Traktat* (Hamburg, 1976). Also see R. Spaemann, *Zur Kritik der politischen Utopie* (Stuttgart, 1977), p. 87.

16. O. Marquard, article, "Malum I," in *Historisches Wörterbuch der Philosophie*, vol. 5 (Basel/Stuttgart, 1980), pp. 652–56, and idem, "Vernunft als Grenzreaktion. Zur Verwandlung der Vernunft durch die Theodizee," in H. Poser, ed., *Wandel des Vernunftbegriffs* (Frieburg/Munich, 1981).

17. H. Schelsky, *Die Arbeit tun die anderen. Klassenkampf und Priesterherrschaft der Intellektuellen* (Opladen, 1975), p. 84.

18. B. Brecht, *Gesammelte Werke*, Suhrkamp Verlag together with E. Hauptmann, eds., vol. 12 (Frankfurt, 1968), pp. 375–76.

19. Cf. H. Weinrich, ed., *Positionen der Negativität*, Poetik und Hermeneutik 6 (Munich, 1975), pp. 557ff.

20. Cf. H. von Hofmannsthal, "Ad me ipsum," in *Aufzeichnungen* (a volume of his *Gesammelte Werke in Einzelausgaben*, H. Steiner, ed. [Frankfurt, 1959], pp. 211ff.). This is the step out of the "esthetic" sphere of existence, where everyone is the "sole" being, into "ethical" being for others: "I stand ready to

risk my own life, to play the game of thought with it in all earnest; but
another's life I cannot jeopardize" (S. Kierkegaard, *Philosophical Fragments,*
trans. D. F. Swenson [Princeton, N.J., 1962], p. 6).

21. H. Plessner, *Die verspätete Nation. Über die politische Verführbarkeit bürger-
lichen Geistes* (1939/1959); Frankfurt, 1974), p. 163. Cf. O. Marquard,
"Skeptische Betrachtungen zur Lage der Philosophie," in H. Lübbe, ed., *Wozu
Philosophie?* (Berlin/New York, 1978), esp. pp. 70–74.

22. Cf. H. Cohen, *Ethik des reinen Willens* (Berlin, 1904), p. 502: "Thus modesty
is skepticism's virtue."

23. Cf. M. Heidegger, *Sein und Zeit* (Halle, 1927), pp. 235ff.

24. J.-P. Sartre, *L'être et le néant* (Paris, 1943), p. 638: "le choix que je suis."

25. Following, first of all, M. Kriele, *Theorie der Rechtsgewinnung* (Berlin, 1967);
N. Luhmann, "Status quo als Argument," in H. Baier, ed., *Studenten in Opposition. Beiträge zur Soziologie der Hochschule* (Bielefeld, 1968) (p. 78: "involuntary conservatism as a consequence of complexity"); and H. Lübbe, *Geschichtsbegriff und Geschichtsinteresse. Analytik und Pragmatik der Historie*
(Basel/Stuttgart, 1977), pp. 329ff.

26. D. Hume, *An Enquiry concerning Human Understanding* (1748), section 5:
"custom or habit."

27. Cf. O. Marquard, "Über die Unvermeidlichkeit von Üblichkeiten," in W.
Oelmüller, ed., *Normen und Geschichte* (Paderborn, 1979), pp. 332–42.

28. Cf. M. Hossenfelder, Introduction to *Sextus Empiricus. Grundzüge der pyrrho-
nischen Skepsis* (Frankfurt, 1968), esp. pp. 42ff.

29. H. Blumenberg, *Arbeit am Mythos* (Frankfurt, 1979) (trans. R. M. Wallace,
Work on Myth [Cambridge, Mass., 1985]). Cf. O. Marquard, "Laudatio auf
Hans Blumenberg," in *Jahrbuch der deutschen Akademie für Sprache und
Dichtung 1980/II* (Heidelberg, 1981), pp. 53–56.

30. Cf. O. Marquard, "Einleitung zur Diskussion von H. Blumenberg, 'Wirklichkeitsbegriff und Wirkungspotential des Mythos,' " in M. Fuhrmann, ed., *Terror und Spiel. Probleme der Mythenrezeption,* Poetik und Hermeneutik 4
(Munich, 1971), pp. 527–30.

Translator's Notes

a. The odd phrase, "Auch eine autobiographische Einleitung," presumably al-
ludes to Herder's *Auch eine Philosophie der Geschichte zur Bildung der
Menschheit. Beytrag zu vielen Beyträgen des Jahrhunderts* [Another philosophy of history for the education of Mankind. A contribution to the century's
many contributions] (1774).

b. *Kritischer Rationalismus,* in Germany since the 1960s, has become the rubric
for a group of neopositivists sympathetic to Karl Popper and including Hans
Albert and Ernst Topitsch.

c. A meeting held on the Meissner (a mountain in Hesse) on October 13, 1913, tried to unite the German youth movement under the "Meissner formula." According to this formula the movement intended "to shape its life by its own definition, on its own responsibility, and with inner truthfulness, and to advocate this inner freedom under all circumstances."

d. The "position of possibility" refers to the insistence of philosophical esthetics (in, e.g., Kant, Schiller, and Schelling) on the importance of what has not been "realized," historically. Marquard discusses this "position" in his *Transzendentaler Idealismus, romantische Naturphilosophie, Psychoanalyse* (Cologne, 1987), pp. 142–44. (This book is the Habilitationsschrift [1963] that he refers to later on.)

e. A general change in the atmosphere in intellectual circles in the Bundesrepublik, which became evident in 1977 and came to be called the *Tendenzwende*, signaled the end of the preeminence of the neo-Marxist tendencies that had inspired the student movement of the 1960s and early 1970s.

f. "By means of 'understanding' " = *verstehend*. In the hermeneutic tradition, "understanding" is often contrasted, as the goal of interpretation, to "explanation," as the goal of natural science.

= 2 =

Competence in Compensating
for Incompetence?
(On the Competence and Incompetence of Philosophy)

At a Chinese executioners' competition, the story goes, the second of two finalists found himself in an uncomfortable predicament. His opponent had just completed an exquisitely precise and unmatchable beheading, which he now had to outdo. The suspense was overwhelming. With his keen-edged sword, the second executioner performed his stroke. However, the head of the victim failed to drop, and the delinquent, to all appearances untouched, gave the executioner a surprised and questioning look. To which the executioner's response was: "Just nod, please."

I am interested in what this head thinks, before it makes its last move—because this must resemble the thought that philosophy entertains about itself.

It may seem out of place on a festive occasion, and one held in honor of Mr. Krings, at that, to burden you with details about an executioners' contest. And yet, this is after all a gathering of philosophers, who, I think it can be safely ventured, know what I am talking about. For it is unarguably the case, unless I count myself an exception, that philosophers all have heads—this is after all the tool of their trade, if not their defining attribute. But how firmly do these heads sit? That is really, or at least (and perhaps with even more urgency) metaphorically, the question that has to be faced whenever the issue of the competence or incompetence of philosophy comes up for discussion at the bidding of conference organizers. The more so, when to pose this question is, necessarily, to confront the fate of a decapitated philosophy, a philosophy radically reduced in competence—together with the fact that philosophy evidently continues to hold its head up. I should like to present my considerations on this subject in two segments: In the first, I will take up the issue of philosophy and its reduction in competence; in the second, I will discuss the ways in which philosophy compensates for this reduction.

I

First of all, a few general remarks about philosophy's reduction in competence. What is the meaning of competence in this connection? Initially, I will restrict myself to a notion of competence that is as vague as possible—without making any connections, of a philological kind, with the Latin dictionary, which might locate the word in the general area of rivalry; without making any connections of a juridical sort to the work of legal scholars on the history of their terminology; without making connections of a biological sort with blastema research; without making connections of a linguistic sort with Chomsky; and without making connections of a communicative sort with Habermas. Competence clearly has something to do with responsibility, capability, and readiness; and with the fact that these things overlap. But philosophy in particular has never been something that could automatically be counted on in this regard, for there have always been philosophies that were responsible for nothing, capable of much, and ready for anything. Two thousand years ago, the question whether this diagnosis holds completely and without qualification for all of philosophy would not even have come up for discussion. Today it has. And so history enters the picture right from the start of our deliberation over philosophy and its competence. The competence of philosophy is something that philosophy can only learn from its history. This history, however, tells philosophy that progress has been made in the diminution of its competence: the history of philosophy is the history of the reduction of philosophy's competence.

In the interest of brevity, I will offer a quick, speculative sketch of this historical phenomenon. At first, philosophy was competent in everything; then it was competent in some things; today, philosophy is competent for one thing only—namely, to ackowledge its own incompetence. Here is how it happened. In the course of its laborious and vexed career, philosophy was faced with at least three critical challenges, which left it overextended and, ultimately, spent and exhausted. In short, philosophy was driven out of the running by competent competitors (that is, in the competition for competence). First, there was the soteriological challenge, originating in the Bible; later, there were the technological and the political challenges, in the bourgeois and so-called postbourgeois ages. The soteriological challenge demanded of philosophy that it lead to salvation for humankind. And it became apparent, as Christianity outstripped philosophy, that philosophy was not up to the challenge. So much for its salvational competence: philosophy became a welfare case. For a while, philosophy found work as the *ancilla theologiae,* as the handmaiden to theology. The technological challenge demanded of philosophy that it lead to utility for humankind. As the exact sciences outstripped philosophy, it became apparent that philosophy was not up to the challenge. So much for its technological competence: philosophy became a welfare case. For a while, philosophy was taken on as the *ancilla scientiae,* as the philosophical theory of science. Finally, the political challenge demanded of philosophy that it lead to humankind's well-deserved happiness. But as political praxis outstripped philosophy, whether through its activity, or through its appreciation of the possible, the practicable and the institutionalizable, it became apparent that philosophy was not up to the challenge. So much for its political competence: philosophy became a welfare case. For a while it found work as the *ancilla emancipationis,* as the handmaiden (or else, to avoid discrimination, as the lackey) of emancipation, as the philosophy of history.

In the wake of this succession of difficult challenges and losses, it is doubtful whether it even makes sense to separate out, as a distinct contribution, the component of philosophy that nevertheless was, and perhaps still is, conducive to salvation, technology, and politics. I doubt whether it is more than a pious wish on the part of today's philosophical experts that philosophy should (or if the need actually arose, even could) save common sense and clear-headed reason from those who, as a result of the realities they deal with on an everyday basis, really ought to possess them. Naturally, there are some who regard philosophy as an amulet capable of preventing one from straying down the wrong paths. However—and this is just the reverse of the situation with the horseshoe in the well-known anecdote about Niels Bohr—philosophy has absolutely no effect even if—and especially if—one believes in it.[1]

This brings us to a domain in which philosophy never enjoyed a monopoly on competence in any case: the domain of worldly wisdom. For in giving voice to that wisdom, the poets, at least, were always the rivals of the philosophers. Thus even the special character is threatened that is granted to philosophy when it is defined as the ripe wisdom of those who are not yet old—as the simulation of experience of life for, and by, those who do not yet have any. The biological process attacks this form of competence: philosophers, it happens, age too, even if they occasionally do so unnoticed; and then—this idea runs through my mind only once in a while—they are in a position to replace philosophy with genuinely ripe wisdom, and to dispense with philosophy altogether. To simulate experience of life for those who do not yet have any; to provide ripe wisdom to those who have not gone through the process of aging: this might not only serve as a possible definition of one aspect of philosophy; it is the actual definition of an aspect of the human sciences (*Geisteswissenschaften*) when these have the job of cultivating memory—the very reason why they are currently under attack, which only redounds to their credit. For wherever risks are taken in the name of reform, there is a natural instinct to seek to minimize possible criticism by imposing a ban on remembrance. Does philosophy have a better memory than the humanities? Hardly. And so it happened that in these sciences founded on memory—on which philosophy since the last century staked its claims and hopes in order to make up for its previous losses in competence—there arose a new competitor that now challenges what is perhaps philosophy's last stronghold of competence: the competence to remember. Philosophy is clearly running out of its supply of competencies, with the result that it is on the verge of total incompetence.

This does not mean that philosophy has nothing more to say about all these things; but it has become, overall, a competitor without prospects—at best, the second team, in any particular case. But what good is it to be the second team when the first team is really good, and what is more, is never indisposed? Philosophy has reached a dead end; we are philosophizing after the end of philosophy. "What is to be done?"—here I'm quoting not Lenin but Schiller, in his poem "Teilung der Erde" [The distribution of the earth]. "What is to be done?" asks Zeus, "The world has been given away." But the only constructive suggestion that Schiller's Zeus had to offer was directed at the poets and the poets alone, not the philosophers: to the philosophers, Zeus has nothing to offer in the way of help. And nothing has changed since then. A report on the state of philosophy's competence today consists in an orgy of failing grades.

But really, is this actually the case, and must it be the case? I will be the first to admit that there may be residual competencies for philosophy, perhaps even considerable ones, maybe not even just residual ones, and yet I—I personally—lack the competence to discuss the subject. To do so is not within my sphere of responsibility; I lack the capability to do so—but, if necessary, I am ready to do so, and so let me briefly explain what I mean. To discuss competence is not my responsibility, if for no other reason than out of a consideration for courtesy: for it would be discourteous to give the impression, however faint or remote, that philosophers from Munich need an outsider to assess a competence that they themselves, and perhaps only they, are acquainted with. And why of all things should they need someone born in Further Pomerania, who was forced to become an East Frisian, and passes his dubious existence at the foot of the Vogelsberg, so that he is more likely to be qualified to discuss nonconformistic aspects of South Hessian foundational folklore? Nor am I *capable* of assessing such a competence, and in fact on grounds of incapacity. My work-place is not, after all, an institute for naivety; rather, it is an institute devoted to the search for what is lost,[a] a center for concentrated perplexity. And such a philosopher—let us call him a "sentimental" one—has difficulties with, for example, *theoria,* the attitude that is born from wonder, that unaddressed gratitude for the well-being of the world, which urges the contemplation of the world's good, true, and beautiful order. For our sentimental philosopher makes a poor practitioner of wonder, inasmuch as the only thing that he really wonders at is that he has—for the time being, and improbably—gotten away.

All the same, I am ready to give my views on the remaining competencies of philosophy. This whole process of the loss of competence of philosophy can of course also, in the end, be read quite differently: not as a story about dispossession, but rather as one about disencumbering. For perhaps philosophy's diminishment of responsibilities is in reality a gain in liberties; its ousting can easily signify its release. If there is no longer anything that philosophy has to do, that could mean precisely that it is now permitted to do virtually anything. Thus there may be much left for a disencumbered philosophy to undertake. There are, after all, the tasks its possession of which is still uncontested: the history of philosophy, not to mention logic, though the latter has a symbiotic relationship to mathematics. Symbioses, in general, are important, above all for the philosophy that has oversight of the foundations of the individual sciences. And in these there is, to recall Heidegger's dictum, as much philosophy as there is potential for foundational crises. Crisis-management in foundations is thus an abiding task of philosophy. But who is truly competent here? Pure philosophers? Or the scientists of the various fields in question? The age of pure philosophers has gone by: when they insist on purity, they end up forfeiting philosophy. What, then, is the status of their competence vis-à-vis the foundations of science? Here doubts are both possible and in order.

I will, accordingly, name them freely, partly because it would make a rather poor impression if in this colloquium on philosophy only optimism and celebration were to be heard; and partly out of compositional, and as it were rhythmical, considerations—it is amazing what persons will do (as in the case of the famous weasel) for the sake of a rhyme.[b] My reflections would have no plot and no peripety if at this point I failed to insist on the history of the radical reduction of the

competence of philosophy, and to maintain, emphatically, the following—I repeat: at first, philosophy was competent in everything; then it
was competent in some things; today philosophy is competent for one
thing only—namely, to acknowledge its own incompetence. And if
that is the way things stand, then what is left for philosophy is: absolutely nothing—that is, pure, unadulterated, naked incompetence, as
well as, to cite Socrates, only a single little trifling something, an
admittedly very un-Socratic trifle that, rather than making philosophy
somewhat less problematic, on the contrary makes it 100 percent
problematic; and I should like to name this item, in view of the radical
incompetence that philosophy has arrived at: it is philosophy's competence in compensating for its incompetence.

II

Concerning this, that is, this competence in compensating for incompetence, I should like to make, at this point, two preliminary remarks,
two intermediate remarks, and one concluding remark.

I imagine you will have sensed by now that I have construed my
subject (which as I said was assigned) in a somewhat peculiar way.
What interests me here is not the boundary between the infinitely large
domain of philosophy's incompetence and the infinitely small domain
of its competence, but instead precisely a nonboundary: the blending
of incompetence and competence. And just such a blending, in philosophy, is what I have called its competence in compensating for its incompetence. Now to the preliminary remarks:

1. This competence in compensating for incompetence in philosophy has a lot to do with its incompetence, for compensation is only
necessary where something is missing; and so philosophy's competence at compensating for incompetence is in the first place a symptom
of its incompetence.

2. Philosophy's competence in compensating for incompetence
would be nonexistent if philosophy's incompetence were not complicated by a nostalgia for competence. Everybody talks about nostalgia.
So do I. Philosophy yearns to be something—and it once was something. No amount of self-induced conviction that being something

superfluous is still being something can extinguish this memory. It is true that, as something that is incompetent, philosophy is in fact something superfluous—but it is not straightforwardly superfluous; instead, in its nostalgia for competence, it is something superfluous that is enamored of usefulness—and unhappily enamored. To accept pure superfluousness is hardly something that it could bear. Proof of this is to be found in a phenomenon that is, more than anything else, touching, which is the enthusiasm of philosophers for unpaid sidelines. Man is an active being, philosophers are beings who are active in sidelines: their extraprofessional self-confirmatory activities are currently burgeoning. Philosophers are becoming fetishists of self-management, statisticians of fundamental principles, advisers to new undertakings and to operas, scientific tourists, competitive athletes on the interdisciplinary circuit, architects of plans, statutes, and laws, eminences grises of total transparency (that is, obscurantists of lucidity), mobile psychic facilitators, and (direct and indirect) local politicians, providers of expert opinions and engenderers of paper mountains, secondary salon attractions, and so forth. (In all of this, their well-known weakness for mock jurisprudence is only the secret vengeance of mathematics for its expulsion from the ranks of philosophy: when mathematics disappears from philosophy, it creates the vacuum that is filled by what philosophers and only philosophers take to be juristic logic.) And in every case—in this being-toward-cardiac-arrest, this quest for a circulatory blockage that will serve as proof of their own reality—they accomplish what Gehlen called the flight into overwork: I groan, therefore I am, and a fortiori I am useful.

Philosophers today are the superfluous persons who, in their nostalgia for competence, are unhappily enamored of utility, to the extent of paying court to it through (if need be) unpaid sidelines. So superfluity can operate, for them, as a category of justification, and can (however imperfectly) assuage their spirits, only when a theory of the utility of what is superfluous enters the picture, as for instance in the following way. One extends Veblen's concept of vicarious leisure—an office formerly discharged, among finer folk, by women and domestics—to include philosophers. For frequently philosophers are in fact just that: vicarious idlers in search of finer folk. And that is why philosophers enjoy the company of the powers that be, and even more the company of those who will become the powers that be, and most of all the company of those who will become the powers that be and who are already in power (which of course allows for the limiting case that philosophers should be their own best company). The philosopher—who was admittedly (once again) long ago outdone in this capacity by others—becomes a parasite, in the form of a status symbol. Thus, whether in the orbit of the affluent or of functionaries (the difference, for present purposes, makes no difference), the philosopher is the living symbol of the fact that one person's life is another person's death, that persons live off the suffering of others, that freedom lives off servitude, equality off differences, regard off disregard, fortune off misfortune: this is after all the case. Parasitism is always a matter of course: the essence of philosophy lies in its refusal to allow this proposition to hold good, but nevertheless to be parasitic itself, as a matter of course. Where philosophy has a conscience, this situation torments it; and where it has lost its competencies—but not the impression that it ought to have some—it is immediately, and thus defenselessly, exposed to this torment. What I have called nostalgia for competence articulates this torment and channels it in the direction of compensations. Philosophy consoles itself by wishing, in the face of this torment, either to be itself or not to be itself—with equal desperation in either case. And this means that in its nostalgia for competence philosophy strikes out either the competence or the nostalgia: either it turns into a refugee from competence and seeks nostalgia without competence (that is, an absolute incompetence with fine feelings); or it hugs its competence, seeking a competence without nostalgia (that is, an absolute competence, with the lofty pretensions that go with it). Philosophy hopes to elude the torments of having a conscience by attempting—when that conscience issues its charges—either not to be the party who is being addressed, or else itself to be the one who is doing the addressing; that is, either not to be accountable, or itself to be the accountant. It eludes the scruples of conscience either by being (in various ways) nothing at all, or else by itself being the conscience. Philosophy's compensation for incompetence is, in the face of that possession of a conscience, either a flight into the total incompetence that consists in

philosophy's not being present at all, or a flight into the total competence that consists in philosophy's becoming the absolute conscience
of the world. The philosopher is thus all jester or all judge, either the
one or the other (if these really constitute a disjunction). The two
possible ways of compensating for incompetence that I have just
sketched—philosophy's self-stylization as an absolute court of judgment, or its self-transformation into a nothing that is still just barely
capable of existing (ways that are, at bottom, substitute and successor
forms of two very old factions in philosophy: dogmatism and skepticism)—can be characterized in two brief intermediate remarks:

a. Dogmatism today goes by the name of critique and is, as I said,
the position that asserts philosophy's total competence, by fleeing
from the possession of a conscience into being the conscience. It seems
to me that Freud's theory of the economy of the superego suggests this
rather uncomfortable connection: that those who assume the position
of conscience are spared the need to face their own conscience. It does
not have to work that way, but this does explain why critique frequently exercises an attraction not for its own sake, but rather precisely because of the unburdening effect of the avoidance that it makes
possible.

This is also why talk about unburdening^c is forbidden by the house
rules of critique: it touches too close to home. Critique casts suspicion
on everything, indicts everything, and then sits in judgment on everything. It thus marks a step forward within a tradition: first, in the age
of religion, God sat in judgment over humankind; then, in the age of
theodicy, humankind sat in judgment over God; finally, in the age of
critique, humankind sat in judgment over itself. Thus the judgment of
critique is a self-judgment, and that is hard work; hence, critique
chooses, as a way out, to assume the role not of the defendant but of
the prosecutor. It unburdens itself by judging, so as not to be judged.

Critique is a vacation from the superego, by becoming the superego
that only others have, and that itself has no superego. Thus, for itself,
critique has already escaped the state that in itself, and for critique, is
condemned; so that the others are the condemned state. And critique
escapes absolutely when all condemned states become, in this way,
"the others," and philosophy as critique itself becomes the absolutely

unindictable instance (which human beings, however, cannot really be): the Absolute, which no longer comes in for judgment, because from now on it is the judge, and judges only others. Philosophy once "had" a conscience, but when it is absolutely in advance, it has its conscience behind it; now, instead, it "is" conscience—absolute conscience, in fact.

The institutional consequences, of course, extend far beyond what concerns philosophy as a separate discipline. Its organizing itself into a central institute, as useful as that may be, is not indispensable, for philosophy here, being absolute, is not only central but ubiquitous and omnipresent. Critical philosophy becomes everything, and consequently everything becomes critical philosophy. It dissolves specific substantive domains and their concepts of their objects, and replaces these with emancipatory reflection-concepts, which in essence are instruments both of enticement and of coercion: they entice us toward things progressive, and break down our resistance to them. Critique knows no objects any longer; it knows only relevancies; and thus everything becomes identical: philosophy and politics, utopia and self-preservation, one's chief activity and one's sideline, transparency and opacity, philosophy and the individual sciences, any given discipline and any other (it is only the disciplines themselves that cease to have identity).

Thus the danger arises that the integrated total science of emancipation (which is, as it were, en route from the "idiocy of specialists" (*Fachidioten*) to an integrated—and supposedly "useful"—total idiocy, and from the tyranny of values (*Werte*) to the tyranny of organizational functions (*Stellenwerte*)—that this total science becomes a militant caricature of the System of Identity,[d] in which not only are all cows black, but all academic disciplines are gray, for the same thing is being thought of in all of them and nothing else besides. For this "something else" (the total science thinks) is wicked, both if it is false, and also if it is superfluous—which in practice means, even if it is correct, but not opportune. For what is not in favor of critique is against critique, and thus sinful. Thus at this bacchanalian orgy, in which no member is permitted to stay unintoxicated, it is precisely those who remain sober who are excommunicated. The sciences are once again capable of heresy: once again their research and results are subjected to censorship in the name of salvation. To have liberated us from this condition was the accomplishment of modernity; to rehabilitate it is that of antimodernity. This is the price at which philosophy, under the rubric of critique, dogmatically seeks absolute competence.

   b. The other possibility is the current successor form of skepticism: it is the position that accepts philosophy's total incompetence by fleeing from the possession of a conscience to a more or less tempered irresponsibility, and thus nonpresence, on the part of philosophy or of the philosopher. The relevance of this position in terms of sparing oneself trouble, its productiveness in terms of unburdening, its valency for avoidance are manifest in any case, so that no lengthy discussion of them is required.

This nonpresence can take many forms. The kind of nonpresence that results from being somewhere else is familiar to anyone who is occupied in museum-type activities or is otherwise on the road. But (and this is not a specialty of any particular philosophical school or tendency) one can also not be there in the sense that one is constantly not yet there. One can do this hermeneutically, because the discussion is not yet finished; or dialectically, because the antithesis has not yet arrived; or analytically, because the proposition appears still too immune from refutation; or anthropologically, because it is imperatively necessary first to make another trip to the Bororos; or historically, because everything depends on first investigating Gnosticism more thoroughly; or in the manner of the philosophy of history, because one still has to wait for the base, or for the superstructure, or for the person who will establish absolutely what it is that one has to wait for; or transcendentally, because not all the conditions of possibility are in place, or because too many of them are in place; or esthetically, because the rhythm is not yet right, or only the rhythm is; or rational-reconstructively, because the decisive predicator has still not been introduced by a sufficient consensus; or in the manner of the history of concepts, because so far one has only reached the letter "I"; or just skeptically, because one remains superfluous, and asleep, if one is not occupied just then with one's useful sideline (look out for skeptics who are engaged in their sidelines); and so forth. In cases of absence, like these, the best thing is simply to have all the philosophies, or at least as many as possible, so as always to have precisely the others. Philosophical communication here is the continuation of isolation by other means. Institutionally, the result is the organization of mechanisms that prevent presence.

Here too it is expedient that philosophy should become "central." A center is useful because, where there are faculties or departments, it creates a second obligation of presence, which conflicts with the first one in ways that can be very convenient. Those who are not responsible for philosophy, or for first philosophy, but only for "second philosophy"—the other, the skeptical variety—are impeded in the center by their department, and in their department by the center; and for just this reason, taking the third alternative as best, they can work in their field office for eccentricity—at home, as an *emeritus praecox,* a Sisyphus who must first put together his rock before he begins to roll it, and who must do this with words and ex nihilo.

But, nothing comes from nothing. And the same holds for what these philosophers occupy themselves with: always transforming eager expectancy into nothing. This is, as you know, Kant's definition of laughter. And by the same token, this skeptical philosophy—*tristesse oblige*—is possibly gaiety itself, and even, in this age of the gloomy sciences, the last exile of gaiety—a gloomy one, to be sure: for one who laughs like that has nothing to laugh about.

Wherever—and with this I come to my concluding remark—wherever philosophy is unsure of its competence, wherever it is increasingly incompetent and nostalgic for competence, there it will finally want to be either everything or nothing. I was addressing both possibilities, which are far more identical with one another than either would like. They are compensatory arrangements made under the pressure of reductions in the competence of philosophy: they are compensations for incompetence. Does that justify talk about a competence that philosophy does have: a competence for compensating for its incompetence?

One might think of a use of the term "competence" that stands out in the history of the concept: it is a use found in the ambit of clerical law. There, "competence" is the *terminus technicus* for a kind of clerical alimentation that is a necessary, and therefore nonnegotiable, element in the conduct of a good clergyman's existence. Those who have been through the school of suspicion, from Marx and Nietzsche to Freud, Heidegger, and Adorno, may ask themselves, with learned distrust, why it is that our present-day theoreticians of competence have failed to take note of this usage. For "competence" in this sense can be usefully extended to highlight either the conditions of the possibility of the priesthood (*potestas clavium*) or the minimal appanage of those who take no part in the active life. Such are in fact the two possibilities by which philosophy compensates for its incompetence, which I sketched out earlier: either by holding the absolute power of the keys, or by pursuing a *vita postuma*.

Of course, competence suggests the notion of achievement; but what I described were failures. Perhaps philosophy—I leave this open and say it with some reservation—has no chance today to be anything *but* a failure; or perhaps philosophy's only chance is to confess this to itself. But then philosophy would forsake its authority and would no longer be itself, but would merely be doing, at best, something else instead. When philosophy takes that possibility into account—in that case, it might become humane; for human beings are, after all, the creatures who do something else instead.ᶜ

I was supposed—that is, I was asked—to supply a talk on the competence and incompetence of philosophy. Instead, I gave what I gave instead of that: an antitalk. Malraux in his *Antimémoires* threw open the question whether memoires have to exhibit resemblance in an age when even portraits are no longer meant to resemble. In recalling the basic right to ineffability, in this age of total transparence, I will extend Malraux's question not to lectures in general, but to this lecture.² And I ought, moreover, to make perfectly clear that I am bringing my talk to a close, lest you should be struck by the appalling thought that, in obedience to some sort of principle of eternal recurrence, I might start it all over again when I conclude it in the following way:

At a Chinese executioners' competition, the story goes, the second of two finalists found himself in an uncomfortable predicament. His opponent had just completed an exquisitely precise and unmatchable beheading, which he now had to outdo. The suspense was overwhelming. With his keen-edged sword, the second executioner performed his stroke. However, the head of the victim failed to drop, and the delinquent, to all appearances untouched, gave the executioner a surprised and questioning look. To which the executioner's response was: "Just nod, please."

I am interested, I said, in what this head thinks, before it makes its last move—because this must resemble the thought that philosophy entertains about itself. I suppose you must be wondering, after bearing with me for the past forty-five minutes or so, when will he finally nod?

Notes

1. All philosophically pregnant anecdotes in our day that have to do with natural scientists tend to become Niels Bohr anecdotes. The one I am referring to goes as follows: Niels Bohr is paid a visit at his ski chalet, over whose door a horseshoe is attached. The guest points to the horseshoe and asks Bohr, "Do you, a natural scientist, actually believe in that?" Bohr: "Of course not. But I've been assured that horseshoes work even if you don't believe in them."

2. A lecture that, strictly speaking, violates the self-interest of the profession, by presenting philosophy as something toward which—both in its dogmatic form, as critique, and in its skeptical form, as the position that consists in nothingness—one should at present adopt a skeptical attitude. But looking at it indirectly, the opposite is in fact the case, especially because the lecture can after all also be read as a dialectic of philosophy's failures, which is meant to provoke an analytic of its accomplishments. For what an unshakeable vitality is after all demonstrated by philosophy as a faculty by the mere fact that it can afford to employ, as its cheerleader on a representative occasion, the member of the guild who is (where his chief activity is concerned) its most notorious defeatist!

Translator's Notes

a. Marquard is one of the directors of the Center for Philosophy and the Foundations of Science at the Justus Liebig University in Giessen. So "what is lost" is, perhaps, "the foundations." "Naive" versus "sentimental," the contrast he plays on in this passage, stems from Schiller's *Über naive und sentimentalische Dichtung* (1795/96), in the first of which the poet "is nature," whereas in the second he "seeks" nature. Further Pomerania was a Baltic province most of whose German inhabitants migrated (or were deported) westward in 1945 and 1946 when it became part of Poland.

b. The protagonist of Christian Morgenstern's poem, "Das aesthetische Wiesel . . . sass auf einem Kiesel . . . um des Reimes willen."

c. *Entlastung,* "unburdening," is a key concept in Arnold Gehlen's philosophical anthropology, for which the advocates of Critical Theory (who are the main targets of Marquard's discussion of "critique," here) have little sympathy. In other contexts in this work I have sometimes translated *Entlastung*—which is a word that Marquard uses frequently—as "disencumbering."

d. The *Identitätssystem* was Schelling's term for his first philosophical synthesis, laid out in his *Darstellung meines Systems der Philosophie* (1801). It was compared to "the night in which all cows are black" by Hegel in the Preface to *The Phenomenology of Mind* (1807).

e. On "doing something else instead," see the essay on "The Question to which Hermeneutics is the Answer," sections 3 and 4.

=3=

Indicted and Unburdened Man
in Eighteenth-Century Philosophy

The philosopher is not the expert, but the expert's stunt man: his double in dangerous situations. At any rate, that is exactly my role here in connection with the analysis of the redefinition of man in the eighteenth century. From which I draw the following conclusion: because a stunt man who does not act· recklessly is worthless, in what follows, I will act recklessly. Following this precept, I will treat my theme in five sections, as follows: (1) new philosophies; (2) *Homo compensator;* (3) overtribunalization; (4) the escape into unindictability; (5) the flight into being the world's conscience, and the collapse of that flight. So, to the matter at hand—to man.

New Philosophies

Perhaps you have already been forewarned that I always come to the subject of theodicy in one way or another. And indeed, how lucky I am that Leibniz published the book of this title in 1710—that is, during the eighteenth century.[1] Otherwise, despite all my efforts, I would find myself—with this talk—in front of the society for the study of what is for me the wrong century.[a] But as it is, it is permissible for me to speak of theodicy here, too—as indeed I will, though not until later.

I will begin with this observation: as a rule, the change in the anthropological picture in the eighteenth century—the redefinition of man that takes place there—is more concealed than revealed by the explicit definitions of man provided by the philosophical experts, who almost without exception hold (though sometimes in very sophisticated ways) to traditional formulations. Therefore, we must be on the lookout for other phenomena the consideration of which will help to reveal this redefinition. One of these phenomena in the eighteenth-century is the *rapid rise of new philosophical disciplines* with *scienza nuova* appeal, and their advancement to the role of official fundamental philosophies. One might well surmise that these disciplines advance because they insist on something about man that the traditional, long-established philosophies were incapable, or were no longer sufficiently capable, of affirming.

At first glance, it seems that this process chiefly affects the second half of the century. Whatever else it may be, the eighteenth century is the century of the "saddle period," to bring into play here a concept that was coined by Reinhart Koselleck.[2] Its purport is that shortly after 1750, a variety of significant things all happen at the same time, as the history of concepts can clearly demonstrate (just as ticks always land on butyric acid, so, too, conceptual historians always land on 1750). At this point in time, the history of concepts also documents, above all, the advancement of the new philosophies that I referred to.

This is the point at which the *philosophy of history,* under that name, comes into being. Summing up his previous work on this subject in his article "Geschichte/Historie" in *Geschichtliche Grundbegriffe* [Fundamental historical concepts], Koselleck, again, has shown that beginning precisely with the introduction, entitled "Philosophie de l'histoire" (1765), to Voltaire's *Essai sur les moeurs* [Essay on morals] (1756),[3] books begin to appear in rapid succession launching this philosophical discipline and elevating it, since Fichte at the latest, to a philosophy that plays the role of a fundamental philosophy, and puts forward man as someone who could not exist in the old metaphysics: as *homo progressor et emancipator* [progressive and emancipatory man].

But—and this state of affairs should give us food for thought—the philosophy of history is by no means the only new philosophy at this point in time. For there is also *philosophical anthropology*. It exists, of course, since about 1600.⁴ But it is not until the eighteenth century—when Gottfried Polycarp Müller held the first series of lectures on anthropology as such in Leipzig in 1719—that, as Mareta Linden has well demonstrated in her recent *Untersuchungen zum Anthropologiebegriff des 18. Jahrhunderts* [Investigations of the concept of anthropology in the eighteenth century],⁵ philosophical anthropology, from the middle of the century on, secures its first definitive breakthrough as a quasi-vitalistic reply to the Cartesian dualization of man. Anticipated by Struve's *Anthropologia naturalis sublimior* [Higher natural anthropology] of 1754, from (especially) Platner's *Anthropologie für Ärzte und Weltweise* [Anthropology for doctors and philosophers], which appeared in 1772 (the initial year of Kant's anthropology lectures and the year in which Herder's essay on the origin of language appeared), to Wilhelm von Humboldt's "Plan einer vergleichenden Anthropologie" [Plan of a comparative anthropology] of 1795,⁶ there is a boom in philosophical anthropology, which puts forward man as someone whom, even in the most recent form of the old metaphysics—in dualistic Cartesianism—man was not allowed to be: as the psychosomatic "whole person"—that is, not simply *res cogitans* (a thinking thing), but *homo naturalis et individualis* (natural and individual man).

Finally, at the same time, we find the emergence of *philosophical esthetics*. Its initiating book appears in 1750: Baumgarten's *Aesthetica*, which rehabilitates sense experience—*aesthesis*. The latter's imaginative productivity will be the touchstone of the philosophy of the fine arts, which—after the importation of Burke's "Ideas" (1757), also "on the sublime," by Kant's "Beobachtungen" [Observations] on that topic, from 1764 to 1790—inclines Kant's *Critique of Judgment* toward the central philosophical position that is perfected in Schiller's *Ästhetische Brief* [Esthetic letters] in 1794 and in Schelling's transcendental system in 1800.⁷ By becoming the central dominating philosophy, philosophical esthetics puts man forward as something that man was not allowed to be under the sign of the metaphysical and exact primacy of the rational and the efficient: as *homo sensibilis et genialis* (sensual and genial man).

Now, after these three indications, my question is: *Why do these three new philosophies*—at least these three: the philosophy of history, philosophical anthropology, and philosophical esthetics—*advance simultaneously and why, precisely,* true to the saddle-period, so to speak, *shortly after 1750?* Perhaps it is permissible, with a bow to Oetinger, to move a late phenomenological concept forward into the eighteenth century[8] and say that we are dealing here with philosophies that provide new definitions of man which *attempt to compensate for a human loss of "life-world,"* and a loss that is specific to the middle of the century. The more detailed characterization of this impairment of the life-world can vary: it can proceed, for example, by way of the (*sit venia dicto*) Carl Schmitt-Lepenies thesis of the birth of morally hypertrophic or melancholic bourgeois interiority out of the spirit of the inhibition of action by absolutism's excess of order;[9] or by way of Koselleck's supplementary thesis that redefinitions become necessary because, with the new acceleration of social change, "experience" and "expectation" begin to diverge.[10] Joachim Ritter called this the "divergence between derivation and future" [*Herkunft* and *Zukunft*][11] and developed theorems regarding the compensations that are found for it—theorems of which I will name only one representative here: that the disenchantment of the world by the increasingly "matter-of-fact" attitude that sets in during the eighteenth century is (consistently enough) compensated, at precisely the same time, by the development of the agency of a new enchantment—namely, by the development of the category of the esthetic.[12] I regard all these theses as plausible and I do not intend to put them into question. All I wish to do here is to try to supplement them by pointing out an additional contributory reason for the simultaneous innovations sketched above—the innovations of the philosophy of history, philosophical anthropology, and philosophical esthetics—with this thesis: *The simultaneous development, around 1750, of these philosophical formations that redefine man is part of the phenomenon of a flight from the "overtribunalization" of the human world, which sets in at just that time; these formations are attempts to compensate for this overtribunalization by an "escape into unindictability."*

Homo Compensator

To elucidate this thesis and make it plausible, I will begin by taking a look at the concept to which I gave a central role in the formulation of my thesis: the concept of *compensation*.[13] The use of this concept does not imply the anachronistic transference of a later category—for example, the one that has entered the consciousness of today's man in the street as a result of the boom in psychoanalysis, in whose context it was developed—to the history of philosophy in the eighteenth century. Rather, the concept of compensation is a descendant of this very history of philosophy in the eighteenth century. More specifically, it is an entry in the balance sheet of the arguments for the defense of God, in (and now we arrive at the key word that I already announced) *theodicy*. Theodicy's inventor, Leibniz, in his justification of God in view of the evils in the world, emphasizes that "the author of nature has compensated these evils with a thousand ordinary and continual amenities." In 1755 the young Kant still attempts to confirm this: "The compensation of evils," he writes in his *Nova dilucidatio* [New elucidation], "is in fact the purpose that the Creator had in view."[14] But in Leibniz's "optimistic" form of theodicy, this is not yet the central argument, but rather only a secondary, flanking theorem. The idea of compensation does not become dominant until the Leibnizian theodicy comes to a crisis, around the middle of the century. Only when the problem posed by evil can no longer be dealt with globally, by the idea of the optimal world, must the question be asked intensively, centrally, and specifically, whether, and where, these evils are balanced out. It is only then that philosophy, drawing up a balance sheet, sets out in search of balances and compensations. Of the several fields in which it searches, I will name four that are of interest:

1. The *individual compensational art* of balancing out evils with goods; this is an art mastered above all by the wise person. Many of the treatises *du bonheur* (of happiness), with the accompanying theme of *sagesse* (wisdom)—which Robert Mauzi has examined for eighteenth-century France[15]—seem to me to fall back, on this subject, on Cicero's thesis in *De natura deorum*, that "sapientes incommoda in vita . . . commodorum compensatione leniant" (the wise mitigate the inconve-

nient things in life by the compensation of convenient things).[16] Because the wise person—as the balanced person—is the one who knows how to live a balanced life, the art of balance becomes decisive: the technique of life that preserves equilibrium through the ability to compensate evils with conveniences.

2. We are interested, too, in the *mechanism of compensation in the world*, which aims at balancing evils with goods. Here philosophy measures and draws up balanced sheets, concluding that the *malheurs*, insufficiently compensated, preponderate (as in Maupertuis's *Essai de philosophie morale* [1749], following Bayle); or that the *bonheurs* preponderate (in 1788, Antoine de Lasalle, advocating this thesis in the tradition of Leibniz, writes in his *Balance naturelle:* "Everything is compensated here below"); or finally that *malheurs* and *bonheurs* hold an even balance. This is the opinion of Robinet (who explicitly asserts his discovery of compensations), in *De la nature* (1761); and, in 1763, of Kant in his "Negative Grössen" [Negative magnitudes]; and, in 1788, of Sylvain Maréchal, in his instructional book for royal children entitled *Apologues modernes*. In the *leçon* on *la balance,* Maréchal writes: "Goods and evils remain in a sufficiently complete equilibrium: everything in life is compensated" ("tout est compensé dans la vie").[17]

This thesis of compensation often invokes the doctrine, inspired by Newton, of the origin of reality in the equilibrium of attraction and repulsion. By way of the chapter on dynamics in Kant's *Metaphysische Anfangsgründe der Naturwissenschaft* [Metaphysical foundations of natural science], from 1797 on, this doctrine reaches and stamps even Schelling's theory of indifference in his philosophy of nature—which, after all, is also a philosophy of balance, of equilibrium.[18] Moreover, this thesis of compensation is pointedly recapitulated by Pierre-Hyacinthe Azaïs in his book *Des compensations dans les destinées humaines* [On the compensations in human destinies], before it is picked up again around the middle of the nineteenth century—stochastically by Cournot, emphatically by Emerson, and skeptically by Burckhardt—and then, by way of brain physiology, falls into the hands of psychoanalysis.

Quite consistently, and again in the second half of the eighteenth century, we also find the *compensational program of social reform,* as in utilitarianism, for example. When, despite everything, the outcome of the balance of goods against evils is unsatisfactory, pragmatic progressive measures must be taken to improve the balance in the direction of "the greatest happiness of the greatest number." Helvetius, in 1758, and Bentham, in 1776 and 1789, both proclaim this kind of planned program to *compenser le malheur*.[20] This inevitably leads to the problem of how to indemnify—through compensations—those who do not belong to the "greatest number" and have less than "the greatest happiness." The Chevalier de Chastellux, for example, investigates these questions in his book *De la félicité publique* (1772), and asserts that "happiness is sufficiently compensated" ("le bonheur se compense assez").[21]

These remarks all concern the weak form of the idea of compensation: *despite* the evils, there are goods that compensate for them more or less adequately. But there is also a strong form of the idea of compensation: good comes into being only through evil and in competition with it, a good that could not come about at all without this evil. This is what I should like to call the *bonum-through-malum idea,* which is constructed on the model of the idea of the *felix culpa* (fortunate guilt): only because humans sinned—*malum*—did God come into the world—*bonum*-through-*malum*. Taking up this figure, likewise from the theodicy of Leibniz,[22] Pope, for instance, speaks (in the *Essay on Man*) of "happy frailties" through which "the joy, the peace, the glory of humankind" are realized. And Malthus, too, writes as consolation for the gloomy results of *The Principle of Population:* "There is evil in the world, not in order to produce despair, but rather activity." And this idea is in wide circulation: from Mandeville (there are—*malum*—"private vices," but they are—*bonum*-through-*malum*—"public benefits"), to Herder (man is—*malum*—a stepchild of nature, but—*bonum*-through-*malum*—it is only for this reason that man has language). We find this figure in 1784 in Kant (there are—*malum*—"antagonisms," but—*bonum*-through-*malum*—they accelerate progress), and in 1790 in Schiller (there is—*malum*—the fall, but—*bonum*-through-*malum*—this is precisely how culture arises). In the same year, at the latest—in the *Critique of Judgment*—

this very figure is promoted to the key figure in the thesis of the esthetic of the sublime: granted—*malum*—our senses fail us, but— *bonum*-through-*malum*—it is precisely through this failure that reason demonstrates its power.[23] And so on.

All these indications are intended to show that the idea of compensation is current in the eighteenth century. The second half of the century, in particular, is the true age of compensation; it launches *homo compensator*. Tell me how you compensate, and I will tell you who you are. One might think that just as the guiding formula of the second half of the seventeenth century was the Cartesian "je pense, je suis" (I think, [therefore] I am); in the same way, the guiding formula of the second half of the eighteenth century could have been the formula (which—to my knowledge—remained unformulated), "je compense, je suis" (I compensate, [therefore] I am). This would be the formula of an indirect surrogate optimism in the place where the classical optimism of Leibniz breaks down. Because the global consolation of the idea of the best of all possible worlds slips away, it becomes necessary to mobilize the many intermediate and small consolations that are made possible by the idea of compensation. Which is why this idea becomes central around the middle of the century. But if—and this is the conclusion that I have been working toward— the idea of compensation becomes so current after 1750, we should not be surprised if *there really are compensations* then, as well. Still more: *in this age of philosophies of compensations, there really are compensations provided by philosophies*—at least by the philosophies that, shortly after 1750, come to the fore in a compensatory manner. These include at least those that were named here at the outset: the philosophy of history, philosophical anthropology, and philosophical esthetics. They compensate: of course not just anything at all, but rather a life-world impairment that is, to a degree, distinctly definable, and is specific to the middle of the century. For— and this was my thesis—these new philosophies of the saddle-period compensate, by means of the "escape into unindictableness," for the "overtribunalization" of human life-reality that sets in just at that time. But what is that?

Overtribunalization

The boom in the compensation idea after 1750 is a result of the crisis of the Leibnizian theodicy. Does that also hold for the compensations themselves, the new philosophies of the saddle period? I maintain that the answer is yes. *The advancement of the philosophy of history, philosophical anthropology, and philosophical esthetics is also*—globally speaking—*a result of the collapse of the Leibnizian theodicy.*

The theodicy launched by Leibniz in 1710 is the first new philosophy of the eighteenth century. Among other things, it is new in that it converts philosophy into a legal action: the action of man against God in matters of evil in the world. So the Leibnizian theodicy already contains a redefinition of man: man becomes essentially a party in a legal action—namely, God's *prosecutor*. In this trial God is the accused, the indicted absolute, the absolute defendant. In the Leibnizian form of theodicy, the major supporting argument in God's defense is not, as I have said already, in the first instance the reference to the adequate compensation of evils by goods, but rather is this: creation is the art of the best-possible; therefore, God—like the politician in the "art of the possible": taking account of compatibilities—must put up with and accept evils. The optimal, as end, justifies evils as the condition of its possibility. Therefore, the secret fundamental principle of this theodicy is—*horribile dictu*—the statement: the end sanctifies the means. But in my view, this very principle—the end sanctifies the means—which is supposed to demonstrate "optimistically" the goodness of God, in fact awakens doubt about God's goodness. In a time in which the devil as *genius malignus* (evil genius) was "derealized" from the status of a reality that was believed in to that of a trick of fictional argumentation in the context of systematic doubt, perhaps it was virtually inevitable, in dealing with this now vacant position, that God—specifically by this "optimistic" way of justifying God—should be stylized a bit like the devil. Perhaps it is this that the "disaster of Lisbon" in 1755 (whose literary impact has been studied by, for example, Harald Weinrich)[24] made palpable, thus making a worldwide impression; though philosophical doubts about "optimism" had been expressed much earlier, as is demonstrated by, for example, Philo's position in Hume's *Dialogues Concerning Natural Religion,* which were begun as early as 1751, and by the refutational intention of the question about optimism put forward as early as 1753 for the prize competition of the Prussian Academy.[25]

Henceforth it was natural to think that theodicy does not succeed where—as for Leibniz—God is exonerated *by means of* the creation-principle that "the end sanctifies the means"—but rather that it only succeeds where God is liberated *from* this principle. When this principle, as the principle of creation, nonetheless remains unchallenged, it must ultimately have the following consequence: for the sake of divine goodness, God must be liberated from the role of the creator; to rescue divine goodness, God's nonexistence must be allowed or even insisted upon. This consequence, the inference from God's goodness to God's nonexistence, is drawn—and, not coincidentally, immediately after 1755—by the modern philosophy of history, which instead of God— and, in my opinion, in order to exonerate God—proclaims man as the creator, declaring reality to be the creation that, as Vico was the first to think, man himself can make: history. The philosophy of history is the completion of theodicy, emerging out of a crisis of theodicy and consummating it through its radicalization; it completes theodicy by acquitting God on the grounds of the most proven innocence possible: namely, the innocence of nonexistence. Through this atheism *ad maiorem Dei gloriam* (to the greater glory of God),[26] man inherits God's functions: not only the function of creator, but also (and this is important here), for that very reason, the function of the one who is indicted by theodicy. Then the philosophy of history has the following consequence: philosophy remains a legal action, and man remains the absolute prosecutor, but at least one thing has changed: from now on, in the same case (the case of the evils in the world), man instead of God, is the absolute defendant. This is, in my opinion, the decisive redefinition of man that the radicalization of theodicy into the philosophy of history, shortly after 1750, brings with it, and to which I should like to draw attention here: Man becomes *the absolute defendant.* This is—*in nuce*—the condition that I have described as the "overtribunalization" of the reality of human life: *that from now on, man, absolutely indicted for the world's evils before a permanent tribunal in which humankind itself is both*

*prosecutor and judge, falls subject to an absolute pressure for self-
justification, an absolute legitimation-compulsion.*

Is this definition of man really new? At first glance, it seems quite
old, at least as old, in fact, as Christianity. There, too, man is absolutely accused—namely, by the absolute, by God: because of sin. But in
Christianity, this absolute indictment is at the same time absolutely
moderated: by God's *grace*. In Christianity, man precisely does not fall
subject to the absolute pressure for self-justification, because that
justification—which Christianity does not expect man to provide, because man is incapable of that—has already taken place: through
God's deed, the divine redemption that Christianity conveys. It was
only for this reason that the root of the autobiographical efforts in
antiquity—namely, the need for an apology (impressively underscored
by Manfred Fuhrmann in the eighth "Poetik und Hermeneutik" ses-
sion)[27]—could, from the time of Augustine, be detached from the
license to confess one's own neediness and particularity. Only in
Christianity—under the protection of grace—can autobiography tend
toward candor and a capacity for individuality; for only in Christianity—despite sin, and because of God's act of redemption—is man
granted the state of grace, which is a secondary freedom from the need
for justification.[28] *In Christianity, man is spared by grace this status of
the absolute accused.* This changes in modernity; at the latest, at that
moment in the beginning of the eighteenth century when, with God as
the absolute defendant in theodicy, man advances to the position of the
absolute prosecutor. *The absolute indictment then becomes merciless,*
for there is no grace; and foremost, simply because it is not for man to
grant clemency to God. When radicalized theodicy, the philosophy of
history, makes man the absolute defendant instead of God, the absolute indictment remains merciless, without grace.

This, *the loss of grace,* is a specifically modern operation, a decisive
contributing cause of the overtribunalization of the reality of human
life. Because the absolute indictment for the evils of the world befalls
man mercilessly and places man mercilessly under the total pressure
for self-justification, this indictment becomes humanly unendurable
and unliveable. Leibniz's question to the creator: "Why is there something rather than nothing?"[29] is not only reformulated juridically, in

the manner of theodicy, as the accusatory question: With what right does anything exist and is anything accepted rather than nothing? Beyond that, and beyond the *quaestio juris* of Kant's "transcendental deduction," which concerns only categories (by what right are any a prioris accepted, rather than none?),[30] this question is finally intensified and ubiquitized as the absolute, merciless accusation addressed to everyone: By what right do you exist at all, rather than not, and by what right are you as you are, rather than otherwise? Under the pressure of this question, every human being must, from now on, be ready, continuously and in toto, to present an accounting; every person—as a secularized *causa sui* (self-causing agent)—bears the total burden of proof, with no pardon, that he or she is permitted to be, and permitted to be as he or she is. The exclusive task of human life becomes: having to live, before a permanent tribunal in which man acts at once as both prosecutor and judge, an exculpation for the fact that one exists, rather than not, and that one is as one is, rather than otherwise.

"Tribunalization" is my name for the rising trend in which this total legitimation-compulsion for everyone emerges, around 1750, through the radicalization of theodicy into the philosophy of history. And the fact that this compulsion becomes total and merciless, devoid of grace, I call the *overtribunalization of the reality in which humans live*. This compulsion—of which the prime example in reality is of course the tribunal mania of the French Revolution—functions for human beings as a threat to and a loss of their life-world, for—and I repeat—it is unendurable, it is unliveable.

The Escape into Unindictability

As a result, precisely, of this overtribunalization and its unliveability, there emerges an enormous need for unburdening (*Entlastung*), an "antitribunal" need to be freed from the demand for self-justification: *overtribunalization (malum) compels (bonum-through-malum) the escape into unindictability*. This is why those new philosophies now become important ("now" being shortly after the middle of the century), which, in a compensatory manner, insist upon the qualities in man that have the effect of resisting, causing problems for, and reject-

ing the absolute accusatory pressure of the question of total legitimation. These philosophies are—for the philosophy of history is, as I
have already suggested, initially a somewhat different case—above all
philosophical anthropology and philosophical esthetics. They were
needed, and directly they were there: as philosophies of man in search
of unburdening. I think the time has come to interpret both of them as
philosophies of the escape into unindictability. With no claim to total
completeness, I will briefly indicate here seven pertinent points that
(even before the later arts of avoiding responsibility) these philosophies in particular put forward—partly the one, partly the other, and
partly both together.

1. Part of the escape into unindictability is that man marks out the
limits of human self-causality, and thus also marks out the human
qualities in relation to which questions of legitimation are meaning-
less. In a posttheological context, the most essential of these limits is
that which, in humankind itself, is *nature:* philosophical anthropology
is successful in the second half of the eighteenth century precisely
because—in contrast to what man "as a freely active being makes of
man, or can or should make of man"—it thematizes and stresses,
instead, "what nature makes of man."[31] That is, philosophical anthropology's success is not due to its "moral" or "pragmatic," but rather
to its "physiological" program: as the philosophical agent of a *turn
toward nature,* for the purpose of the escape into unindictability.

2. Part of the escape into unindictability is meeting *the need for
anonymity* that is inevitably produced by the burden of the public
exposure that goes with being obliged to justify oneself totally. This
passion for situations in which one is untraceable and unidentifiable,
and thus inaccessible for questions of legitimation, is satisfied by *virgin
nature,* which offers a holiday from the accused ego; here one can lie
low, in one's flight from the identifying clutches of the total demand
for justification. *The boom in the longing for virgin nature* (a longing
that, again, is established shortly after 1750 by, for instance, Rousseau) *is a boom in this unburdening effect;*[32] it is part of the escape into
unindictability.

An additional revealing point here (among others) is that just as
Augustine could achieve the old candor of his *Confessions* only under

the protection of grace, so Rousseau could achieve the *nouvelle sinceri-té* of his *Confessions* only under the protection of this nature. The positive value assigned to virgin nature is a profane compensation for the loss of grace.

3. Part of the escape into unindictability is the boom in *individuality*, which is encouraged by the development of the doctrine of "characterization" within the philosophical anthropology of the second half of the eighteenth century, and reinforced by the genesis of the sense of history.[33] *Individuum est ineffabile* (the individual is ineffable); and for just this reason—because the demand for justification cannot reach the individual's ineffable individuality—human beings as individuals are inaccessible for questions of legitimation, which is precisely why they must become individuals. *From the middle of the eighteenth century on, the rapid rise of "individuals" is the rapid rise of their ineffability,* as an answer to the hypertrophy of the legitimation-compulsion: as an escape into unindictability.

4. Part of the escape into unindictability is the *enthusiasm for absence:* persons are unindictable when they *travel,* and are partially so even when they are preparing for or working up the results of a journey. Hence the fascination with the activities of anthropological ethnologists, of the Forsters, Bougainvilles, and Blumenbachs. When being at home increasingly comes to mean the necessity of living out excuses for oneself before a tribunal, foreign lands and peoples beckon as opportunities not to be at home; which is why travel literature, also, immediately blossoms, from the fictional—Sterne's *Sentimental Journey*—to the massive collections of travel descriptions that begin to appear in Germany in 1764.[34] Here there are not only the voyages into unknown space, but also the voyages in time: the historiographer's mental excursion into the past, into remote antiquity. The identity of the foreign and of prehistory is foreign prehistory; so by the same token, shortly after 1750, the monomyth of a single history, with its passion for tribunals, is countered (by, for example, Heyne and Zoëga)[35] with an opposing interest in the polymyths especially of exotic, nonoccidental, preclassical, and oriental mythology. Foreign lands, prehistory, and foreign prehistory—these are all opportunities to be on a journey or to have emigrated—that is, to be unindictable because one is absent. *The eigh-*

teenth century is a century of travel, as a form of escape into unindictability and to that extent—nota bene—the anticipator of many a later
travel mania that has the same motivation, all the way up to today's
tourism, and "scholarly tourism." In the present day, the more time
researchers must spend in the tribunals, which the administrative bodies
of the reformed universities have become, the more irresistible absence
through travel becomes. Which is why one travels, for example, to
Wolfenbüttel.

5. Part of the escape into unindictability is the surrogate absence
that is employed by those who chronically remain at home: this is
sickness. Anthropological nosologies and the "birth of the clinic"[36] (in
the age of the death of metaphysics) make sickness an opportunity for
unburdening oneself that is as painful as it is attractive. Because, in this
way, *man becomes, representatively, a patient,* there is a boom in medical anthropology in the second half of the eighteenth century; and to a
significant extent philosophical anthropology, too, is written for and by
medical doctors. Insanity becomes the most fascinating form of disease;
when, under the sign of overtribunalization, man is increasingly held
responsible for everything, man begins to favor, compensatorily, *the
wished-for state of irresponsibility (Unzurechnungsfähigkeit*—that is,
insanity). The positive evaluation given to insanity[37]—also in the context of the theory of genius, in philosophical esthetics—is an escape into
unindictability.

6. Another part of the escape into unindictability is the *genesis of
the esthetic.* Along this route to the estheticization of art—from rationality to "sensibility," from the normative to the original, from *imi-
tatio* to the genius—exactly in the second half of the eighteenth century, phantasy becomes the noblest productive power, and taste the
leading receptive one. In her *There is No Disputing about Taste* (written under the direction of Prof. Fabian), Hannelore Klein sums up:
" 'Taste' is . . . an eighteenth-century concept."[38]

Taste rapidly rises to prominence precisely at this time precisely
because it does not get involved in disputation, or in legitimation: it is
a *refuge of human freedom from the need for justification,* a resur-
rection of the self-evidence (which is otherwise lost) of matters of

course. As a holiday from the tribunal, art becomes esthetic; as art becomes autonomous, and its inaccessibility becomes institutionalized, the work of art becomes, perhaps most of all, the thing in the face of which the question, "With what right . . . ?" falls silent. From now on the esthetic realm becomes exceedingly important precisely on account of its resistance to demands for legitimation. Precisely in the second half of the eighteenth century, the art of the "genius" advances to the status of a central organ of the life-world, and the artist, as the original "outlaw," becomes the exemplary human being: with a view to the escape into unindictability.

7. And finally, another part of the escape into unindictability, precisely in the second half of the eighteenth century, is the attempt to establish legal boundaries to the absolute demand that persons should justify themselves: the *conception and proclamation of fundamental human rights,* which are meant to protect (to the extent that this can be done by means of law) freedom from the demand that persons should justify their existence and their being the way they are.[39] Precisely man's metamorphosis into the absolute defendant necessarily leads to the attempt to define and guarantee borders within which man is never a defendant.

We have become accustomed to regarding these fundamental rights, which ward off the legitimation-compulsion, as results of the progress that is promoted by the philosophy of history; but it is time to try to conceive them—quite to the contrary—as preventive measures taken to protect against the tribunalizing consequences of the philosophy of history: that is, as phenomena of the escape into unindictability.

These seven observations, which undoubtedly could and should be added to, were meant to advance the idea that anthropology and esthetics—not only they, but they in particular—became successful after 1750 because just at that point, through the overtribunalization of the life-world, absolutely *indicted* humanity acquired an urgent need to become *unburdened* humanity. Philosophical anthropology and philosophical esthetics were promoted at the same time as agents of man's—compensatory—escape into unindictability.

The Flight into Being the World's Conscience, and the Collapse of this Flight

The philosophy of history, I have said, is, to begin with, a different case: it is itself the philosophical *agent* of overtribunalization. I nevertheless think, as improbable as this might sound at first, that it is also at the same time the agent of an escape into unindictability—of the escape accomplished by *raising tribunalization to a higher power*. In this form, German Idealism, which understood itself as a parallel action to the French Revolution,[40] made the philosophy of history the fundamental and highest philosophy. Fichte, above all, who radicalized Kant's theory of the conscience as autonomous, in his *Foundation of the Complete Science of Knowledge* of 1794 (a book that was published in the eighteenth century), specified the "history of the human spirit"[41] as the process in which the I posits itself by setting itself off from the not-I, and indeed to the point that it becomes the absolute.

As I emphasized earlier, the philosophy of history, which is a theodicy radicalized by the release of God from God's duties, differs from the classical theodicy in that, in regard to the evils of the present world, it makes man instead of God, the *absolute defendant*. But at the same time—and I have to make up now for not having emphasized this earlier—it agrees with the classical theodicy in making man the *absolute prosecutor*. And it is precisely this that offers the opportunity for a special kind of unburdening, which is seized by the version of the philosophy of history that Fichte presents in his *Science of Knowledge*. History is the procedure that makes possible for humankind a division of labor, or so to speak a division of life, in relation to this double role as the object and the subject of the absolute indictment. Thus humankind (little by little) escapes from the role of the absolute defendant by (little by little) making the role of the absolute prosecutor its exclusive role. The object of the accusation is, then, no longer the I, but rather becomes the not-I, to exactly the extent that the I itself becomes exclusively the subject that does the accusing. Persons are indeed still absolute defendants, but only the *other* persons—because all that one is oneself, now, is the absolute prosecutor. Sometimes I call this the "Neomanichaeism" of the established philosophy of history: there is a parting of the ways between man the creator (here in the role of the defendant), and man the redeemer (here in the role of the prosecutor). Under the pressure of overtribunalization, history is this "flight forward" into absolute indicting, which leaves *being* absolutely indicted behind it as the condition of those who are not the avant-garde. The law of motion (baptized the "dialectic" only shortly thereafter) of the historical avant-garde is that it deals with the world's evils by fleeing into the bad conscience that it *becomes* for the others in order to let the others *have* it, so that it no longer has to *have* it itself. One escapes the tribunal by becoming it. The vast expenditure of moral indignation that is generated here is only insurance against what this escape precariously enables one no longer to be, but only (from now on) to *judge*.

Thus, history—for the philosophy of history—is *the permanent flight from having a conscience into being the conscience.*[42] In this sense, as humankind's absolution of itself by escalating the legitimation-pressure on other persons, history, too, is an escape into unindictability—the escape that at the same time infinitely intensifies indictability, that is, overtribunalization—for others. Thus, at this price, the philosophy of history, too, turns indicted man into unburdened man. And make no mistake: it is precisely this unburdening effect that makes the philosophy of history successful. Thus it, too, promotes a new definition of man; but this new definition seems in fact to define man out of existence. For the situation seems, in fact, to be this: just as theodicy was made consistent by the negation of God, so the philosophy of history is made consistent by the negation of man; it breaks man in two, into the merciless absolute and its absolute enemies. When it does not remain anthropologically and esthetically moderate, but rather becomes radical as the philosophy of history, the redefinition of man in eighteenth-century philosophy *defines man in a way that leads to the end of man's humanity.* This process reaches far beyond the eighteenth century. I have only sketched it here, and it is not my business to pursue it further on this occasion.

In conclusion, then, just one more thing: he who digs pitfalls for others, can fall into them himself. He who, like the philosophers of history, persistently demonstrates to his fellows the dialectical art of always accusing and letting only the others be guilty should not be surprised if his fellows finally learn this art and, turning the tables, apply it in their turn—to the philosophers of history themselves and finally, by the principle of the clan's liability for its members, to philosophers as a whole. In 1818 de Bonald wrote: "Today, it is an article of faith that the philosophers of the eighteenth century have nothing to do with our catastrophies. . . . I at least would prefer, for the honor not only of philosophy, but also of the nation, to give both a bit more blame." Helmuth Plessner used this sentence as the motto of his *Die verspätete Nation* [The belated nation];[43] and the most successful expropriator of the thesis of Plessner's book, Georg Lukács, condensed it, in his *The Destruction of Reason,* into the statement that there is no innocent philosophy (which was undoubtedly more honest, by one philosophy, than he meant it to be).[44]

The transformation of the thesis of philosophy's guilt into the common property of public opinion succeeded because two things had occurred with respect to philosophy. First—and this was accomplished essentially in the eighteenth century—philosophy was transformed into a special affair; from having been "the science of everything possible" (Christian Wolff, 1705), it became the special affair of "critique" (Kant, 1781).[45] Secondly—and this was accomplished essentially in the nineteenth century—because philosophy, which as the philosophy of history promised the fulfillment of all hopes, was necessarily disappointing, this disappointment (*Enttäuschung*) *by* philosophy inevitably led to the disillusionment (*Enttäuschung*) *of* philosophy: to the critique of ideology.[46] Ideology critique can become popular because, in its turn, it promises unburdening: from now on, the nonphilosophers are unburdened man for the unmasked and accused man is now—in many domains—very much the philosopher.

Thus philosophy's situation becomes the opposite of everything that, as the philosophy of history, it intended: it is the situation of the failure of the flight into being the world's conscience, of the collapse of the absolute, of the reversal of the direction of accusation. Thus, at the end of this operation—that is to say, today—the philosopher becomes the handy, easy-care, no-wrinkle, all-purpose scapegoat. As a well-trained all-around alibi, he belongs, from now on, to everyman's prophylactic routine of self-exculpation.[47] Of course philosophers, in this situation, can be put to work in a variety of ways—they are, as it were, polyvalent. For example, they can professionalize their new status, and perform—in this age of scholarly tourism—as traveling experts in unburdening, specialists in risky tasks, and transcendental stuntmen, who act as doubles for real experts in cases where it could be dangerous for them to act themselves: for example, for experts on the eighteenth century facing the question of the redefinition of man in the philosophy of that period. With this concluding remark, I wanted not only to bring together the past and the present, but also to underscore expressly, once again, the force of what I intimated at the outset: that this, my expertise, was not an authentic expertise, but rather a stand-in expertise—that is, the product of a stunt man, a double: *doublé*.

Notes

1. G. W. Leibniz, *Essais de Théodicée sur la bonté de Dieu, la liberté de l'homme et l'origine du mal* (1710), or *Theodicy—Essays on the Goodness of God, the Freedom of Man, and the Origin of Evil* (London, 1951).
2. R. Koselleck, "Richtlinien für das Lexikon politisch-sozialer Begriffe der Neuzeit," *Archiv für Begriffsgeschichte*, 9 (1967), pp. 82, 91, 95.
3. Cf. R. Koselleck's article "Geschichte/Historie," in O. Brunner, W. Conze, and R. Koselleck, eds., *Geschichtliche Grundbegriffe. Historisches Lexikon zur politisch-sozialen Sprache in Deutschland*, vol. 2 (Stuttgart, 1975), esp. pp. 658ff.
4. Cf. Odo Marquard, "Zur Geschichte des philosophischen Begriffs 'Anthropologie' seit dem Ende des 18. Jahrhunderts" (1963), in his *Schwierigkeiten mit der Geschichtsphilosophie* (Frankfurt a.M., 1973), pp. 122–44 and 213–48, and idem, "Anthropologie," in J. Ritter et al., eds., *Historisches Wörterbuch der Philosophie*, vol. 1 (Basel/Stuttgart, 1971), pp. 362–74.
5. M. Linden, *Untersuchungen zum Anthropologiebegriff des 18. Jahrhunderts* (Bern/Frankfurt a.M., 1976) (Studien zur Philosophie des 18. Jahrhunderts, vol. 1), esp. pp. 36ff.
6. K. W. F. Struve, *Anthropologia naturalis sublimior,* (Jena, 1754); E. Platner, *Anthropologie für Ärzte und Weltweise*, vol. 1 (Leipzig, 1772); I. Kant, *Anthropologie in pragmatischer Hinsicht* (1798) (on the dating of the beginning of the seminar, see I. Kant, letter to Markus Herz, in *Werke*, E. Cassirer, ed., vol. 2 [Hildesheim, 1973], pp. 116ff.); J. G. Herder, *Über den Ursprung den Sprache* (1772); W. v. Humboldt, "Plan einer vergleichenden Anthropologie" (1795), in *Werke in fünf Bänden*, A. Flitner and K. Giel, eds., vol. 1 (Stuttgart, 1978), pp. 337–75.
7. A. G. Baumgarten, *Aesthetica* (1750); E. Burke, *A Philosophical Enquiry into*

the Origin of our Ideas of the Sublime and Beautiful (1757); I. Kant, *Beobachtungen über das Gefühl des Schönen und Erhabenen* (1764), or *Observations on the Feeling of the Beautiful and Sublime* (Berkeley: University of California Press, 1965); I. Kant, *Kritik der Urteilskraft* (1790), or *Critique of Judgment (New York: Hafner, 1951); J. C. F. Schiller, Über die ästhetische Erziehung des Menschen* (1794/95), or *On the Aesthetic Education of Man* (Oxford: Clarendon Press, 1967); F. W. J. Schelling, *System des transzendentalen Idealismus* (1800), part 6, in *Sämmtliche Werke,* K. F. A. Schelling, ed., part 1, vol. 3 (Stuttgart/Augsburg, 1860), pp. 612–29; or *System of Transcendental Idealism* (Charlottesville, 1978), pp. 219–33.

8. E. Husserl, *Die Krisis der europäischen Wissenschaften und die transzendentale Phänomenologie* (1935/36), in his *Gesammelte Werke. Husserliana,* vol. 6 (The Hague, 1954), esp. pp. 48ff., or *The Crisis of European Sciences and Transcendental Phenomenology* (Evanston: Northwestern University Press, 1970), pp. 48ff.; see R. Piepmeier, *Aporien des Lebensbegriffs seit Oetinger* (Freiburg/Münich, 1978).

9. C. Schmitt, *Der Leviathan in der Staatslehre des Thomas Hobbes* (Hamburg, 1938); see R. Koselleck, *Kritik und Krise. Ein Beitrag zur Pathogenese der bürgerlichen Welt* (Frieburg/Munich, 1959); W. Lepenies, *Melancholie und Gesellschaft* (Frankfurt a.M., 1969).

10. Koselleck, "Geschichte/Historie," esp. pp. 702ff.; idem, " 'Erfahrungsraum' und 'Erwartungshorizont'—zwei historische Kategorien," in G. Patzig, E. Scheibe, and W. Wieland, eds., *Logik, Ethik, Theorie der Geisteswissenschaften* (Hamburg, 1977), pp. 191–208, esp. pp. 197ff.

11. "The future that begins with society (*Gesellschaft*) has a relationship of discontinuity to what it derives from" (J. Ritter, *Subjektivität* [Frankfurt a.M., 1974], p. 27); see J. R., *Metaphysik und Politik* (Frankfurt a.M., 1969), esp. pp. 212ff., 338ff.

12. See Ritter, *Subjektivität,* esp. pp. 141ff.

13. See Marquard, "Kompensation," in J. Ritter, et al., eds., *Historisches Wörterbuch der Philosophie,* vol. 4 (Basel/Stuttgart, 1976), pp. 912–18; idem, "Kompensation: Überlegungen zu einer Verlaufsfigur geschichtlicher Prozesse" in K. G. Faber and C. Meier, eds., *Historische Prozesse (Theorie der Geschichte. Beiträge zur Historik, vol. 2 [Munich, 1978], pp. 330–62); idem,* "Glück im Unglück. Zur Theorie des indirekten Glücks zwischen Theodizee und Geschichtsphilosophie," in G. Bien, ed., *Die Frage nach dem Glück* (Stuttgart, 1978), pp. 93–111.

14. "L'auteur de la nature a compensé ces maux . . . par mille commodités ordinaires et continuelles," G. W. Leibniz, *Théodicé,* in *Die philosophischen Schriften,* C. I. Gerhardt, ed. (Berlin, 1875–90), vol. 6 (repr. Hildesheim, 1961), p. 409; "Nam ea ipsa malorum . . . compensatio . . . est proprie ille finis, quem ob oculos habuit artifex" (I. Kant, "Principiorum primorum cogni-

tionis metaphysicae nova dilucidatio," in *Gesammelte Schriften*, Akademie
ed., vol. 1 [Berlin, 1902], p. 405).

15. R. Mauzi, *L'idée du bonheur dans la littérature et la pensée françaises au XVIIIᵉ siècle* (Paris, 1960; 3rd ed., 1967).

16. Cicero, *De Natura deorum*, 1,21; see idem, *Tusculanae disputationes*, 5,95.

17. P. Bayle, *Réponse aux questions d'un Provincial* (1704), in *Oeuvres diverses* (The Hague, 1727–31), vol. 3, esp. pp. 650–51; P. L. M. de Maupertuis, *Essai de philosophie morale* (1749); Leibniz, *Theodicée*, pp. 266–67; A. de Lasalle, *Balance naturelle* (1788); J. B. Robinet, *De la nature*, (Amsterdam, 1761), p. 3: "D'où résulte un équilibre nécessaire des biens et des maux dans la nature"; cf., e.g., p. 126ff.: "De la Guerre: compensation des maux qu'elle produit" (I thank R. W. Schmidt for the reference); "l'économie universelle," "afin de compenser tout": pp. 105, 109, 133, and many other places; I. Kant, "Versuch, den Begriff der negativen Grössen in die Weltweisheit einzuführen" (1763), in *Gesammelte Schriften*, vol. 2 (1905), pp. 179ff. in connection with p. 197; S. Maréchal, *Apologues modernes, à l'usage du Dauphin, premières leçons du fils ainé d'un Roi* (Brussels, 1788), p. 51 (I thank H. Hudde for the reference).

18. Cf. I. Kant, "Negative Grössen," p. 172 ("Realrepugnanz") and esp. p. 198; *Metaphysische Anfangsgründe der Naturwissenschaft* (1786), in *Gesammelte Schriften*, vol. 4 (1911), p. 523 ("Allgemeiner Zusatz zur Dynamik'); J. G. Fichte, *Grundlage der gesammten Wissenschaftslehre* (1794), in *Sämmtliche Werke*, I. H. Fichte, ed., vol. 1 (Berlin, 1845), p. 110 ("negative Grösse"); F. W. J. Schelling, *Ideen zu einer Philosophie der Nature* (1797), in *Sämmtliche Werke*, part 1, vol. 2 (1860), esp. pp. 178ff. and 227ff.; see *Einleitung zu dem Entwurf eines Systems der Naturphilosophie* (1799), ibid., part 1, vol. 3 (1860), esp. pp. 287ff., and *Darstellung meines Systems der Philosophie* (1801), ibid., vol. 4 (1859), esp. pp. 12ff. ("Indifferenz des Subjektiven und Objektiven") and pp. 136ff.: the two opposed forces limit each other, producing the states of balance in which reality consists; this is a kind of *isosthenes diaphonia*, which can obtain not only between dogmatic assertions, but also between forces. Thus in a sense the entire world would be a skeptic.

19. P. H. Azaïs, *Des compensations dans les destinées humaines* (Paris, 1808); A. Cournot, *Exposition de la théorie des chances et des probabilités* (Paris, 1843), chap. 9, par. 103; R. W. Emerson, *Compensation* (1865), in *The Complete Works*, Centenary ed., vol. 2/3 (London, 1904), pp. 91–127. J. Burckhardt, *Weltgeschichtliche Betrachtungen* (1868), in *Gesammelte Werke*, vol. 4 (Stuttgart, 1970), pp. 193–94, or *Reflections on History* (London, 1950), p. 216; A. Adler, *Studie über Minderwertigkeit von Organen (1907)*, or *Study of Organ Inferiority and its Psychical Compensation* (New York, 1917); C. G. Jung, *Zur Psychologie der dementia praecox* (1907), or *The Psychology of Dementia Praecox* (Princeton, N.J., 1974).

20. C. A. Helvetius, *De l'esprit* (Paris, 1758); J. Bentham, *A Fragment on Government* (London, 1776); idem, *An Introduction to the Principles of Morals and Legislation* (London, 1789).

21. Chevalier de Chastellux (anonymous), *De la Félicité publique ou Considérations sur le sort des hommes dans les différentes époques de l'histoire* (Amsterdam, 1772), cited in R. Bury, *The Idea of Progress. An Inquiry into its Origin and Growth* (1932) (New York, 1955), p. 190 (I thank H. Hudde for the reference).

22. Cf. Leibniz, *Théodicée*, p. 108.

23. A. Pope, *An Essay on Man* (1733/34), Ep. II, V. 241ff.; T. R. Malthus, *Essay on the Principle of Population* (1798) [German cited: *Das Bevölkerungsgesetz* (Munich, 1977), p. 170]; B. de Mandeville, *The Fable of the Bees or Private Vices, Public Benefits* (1725); J. G. Herder, *Über den Ursprung der Sprache* (1772), in *Sämmtliche Werke*, B. Suphan, ed., vol. 5 (Berlin, 1895), esp. pp. 27ff.; I. Kant, *Idee zu einer allgemeinen Geschichte in weltbürgerlicher Absicht* (1784), in *Gesammelte Schriften*, vol. 8 (1912), esp. pp. 20ff; F. v. Schiller, "Etwas über die erste Menschengesellschaft nach dem Leitfaden der mosaischen Urkunde" (1790); I. Kant, *Kritik der Urteilskraft* (1790), in *Gesammelte Schriften*, vol. 5 (1908), pp. 244ff, or *Critique of Judgment* (New York, 1951), pp. 82ff.

24. H. Weinrich, "Literaturgeschichte eines Weltereignisses: das Erdbeben von Lissabon" (1964), in his *Literatur für Leser* (Stuttgart, 1971), pp. 64–76.

25. Cf. the dating by G. Gawlick in D. Hume, *Dialoge über natürliche Religion* (Hamburg, 1968), pp. ixff.; on the prize question on optimism ("On demande l'examen du système de Pope, contenu dans la proposition: Tout est bien"), see A. v. Harnack, *Geschichte de Königlich Preussischen Akademie der Wissenschaft zu Berlin*, vol. 1 (Berlin, 1901), p. 404.

26. See O. Marquard, "Idealismus und Theodizee" (1965), in his *Schwierigkeiten mit der Geschichtsphilosophie* (Frankfurt a.M., 1973), p. 65; see also pp. 52–65, 167–78, and 70.

27. See M. Fuhrmann, "Rechtfertigung durch Identität—über eine Wurzel des Autobiographischen," in O. Marquard and K. Stierle, eds., *Identität* (Poetik und Hermeneutik, vol. 8 [Munich, 1979], pp. 685–90).

28. See O. Marquard, "Identität—Autobiographie—Verantwortung (ein Annäherungsversuch)," Marquard and Stierle, *Identität*, pp. 690–99.

29. G. W. Leibniz, *Principes de la nature et de la grace, fondés en raison*, in *Philosophische Schriften*, vol. 6, p. 602: "Pourquoi il y a plustôt quelque chose que rien?", or *Philosophical Papers and Letters*, vol. 2 (Chicago, 1956), p. 1038.

30. I. Kant, *Critique of Pure Reason* (1781) (New York, 1965), pp. 120–21 (B 117–18): "Jurists, when speaking of rights and claims, distinguish in a legal action the question of right (*quid juris*) from the question of fact (*quid facti*); and they

demand that both be proved. Proof of the former, which has to state the right or legal claim, they entitle the *deduction*. . . . Now among the manifold concepts which form the highly complicated web of human knowledge, there are some which are marked out for pure a priori employment, in complete independence of all experience; and their right to be so employed always demands a deduction": that is, a "transcendental deduction"; see what follows.

31. See I. Kant, *Anthropologie in pragmatischer Hinsicht*, in *Gesammelte Schriften*, vol. 7 (1917), p. 119; but philosophical anthropology becomes successful when it *runs counter* to the Kantian program: by turning to nature.

32. J.-J. Rousseau, *Discours sur la question, si le rétablissement des Sciences et des Arts a contribué à épurer les moeurs* (1750); idem, *Julie ou la Nouvelle Héloise* (1761). Here the discovery of "landscape" is not simply a compensation for the loss of naturalness in the increasingly artificial modern world: cf. J. Ritter, "Landschaft. Zur Funktion des Ästhetischen in der modernen Welt (1963)," in his *Subjektivität*, pp. 141ff.; instead, this discovery—like the opportunity (which is functionally equivalent in this respect) for anonymity provided by the great city at the end of the nineteenth and in the twentieth centuries—also offers the possibility of submergence in anonymity in the face of the totally identifying accusatory clutches of "world history as the final judgment." Nature as a refuge (in the form, for example, of untouched landscape) meets the need for solitude that is defined in this way; cf. J.-J. Rousseau, *Le rêveries du promeneur solitaire* (1782).

33. On anthropological "characterization," see Kant, *Anthropologie*, pp. 283ff. W. von Humboldt's *Plan einer vergleichenden Anthropologie* (1795) elevates characterization to the central task of anthropology: cf. Linden, *Untersuchungen*, pp. 139ff. On individuality as the *objectum proprium* of the sense of history, see F. Meinecke, *Die Entstehung des Historismus* (1936) (Munich, 1965), or *Historism. The Rise of a New Historical Outlook* (London, 1972).

34. *Sammlung der besten und ausführlichsten Reisebeschreibungen* (Berlin, 1764ff.); G. Forster, *Neue Geschichte der Land- und Seereisen* (Hamburg, 1781ff.); *Bibliothek der neuesten Reisebeschreibungen* (Berlin, 1786ff.); *Magazin von merkwürdigen neuen Reisebeschreibungen* (Berlin, 1790ff.).

35. See "In Praise of Polytheism. On Monomythical and Polymythical Thinking," in this volume. In general, we can say: what in the seventeenth century was still a danger becomes an enticing temptation; Descartes, for example, warns in *Discours de la méthode* (1637), 1,8: ("*Discourse on method*," in *Philosophical Essays* [Indianapolis: Bobbs-Merrill, 1964], pp. 6–7): "For conversing with the ancients is much like traveling. . . . But when one spends too much time traveling, one becomes at last a stranger at home."

36. See M. Foucault, *Naissance de la Clinique; une archéologie du regard médical* (Paris: Presses Universitaires de France, 1972 [1963]), or *The Birth of the Clinic; an Archaeology of Medical Perception* (New York, 1973).

37. See M. Foucault, *Histoire de la Folie à l'age classique; folie et déraison* (Paris, 1961), or *Madness and Civilization; a History of Insanity in the Age of Reason* (New York, 1965), which stresses the period between 1657 and 1794; on the connections that were made, see O. Marquard, "Über einige Beziehungen zwischen Ästhetik und Therapeutik in der Philosophie des 19. Jahrhunderts," in idem, *Schwierigkeiten mit der Geschichtsphilosophie*, pp. 85–106 and 185–208. The characterization of the artist by "mania," given by Plato in the *Ion* with a polemical intention, becomes contemporary, in modernity, in an affirmative sense, as characterizing the genius (which at the same time also gives insanity a positive value). In this sense, the simultaneity of (for example) Kant's turning to the problems of esthetics and to those of anthropological psychiatry is symptomatic: Kant, "Beobachtungen über das Gefühl des Schönen und Erhabenen" (1764); "Versuch über die Krankheiten des Kopfes" (1764). See also Lepenies, *Melancholie und Gesellschaft*.
38. H. Klein, *There is no disputing about taste. Untersuchungen zum englischen Geschmacksbegriff im 18. Jahrhundert* (Münster, 1967), p. 141; see K. Stierle, H. Klein, and F. Schümmer, "Geschmack," in J. Ritter, ed., *Historisches Wörterbuch der Philosophie*, vol. 3, pp. 444–56. H. G. Gadamer's analysis of the "societal" sense of taste in the eighteenth century (*Wahrheit und Methode*, 1960 [Tübingen, 3rd ed., 1972], pp. 31ff., or *Truth and Method*, G. Barden and J. Cumming, eds. [New York, 1975], pp. 33ff.) also stresses—along with the undemonstrability of taste—i.e., the fact that it lies this side of argumentation—evidence of its resistance to demands for justification; his analysis thus seems to me to support the interpretation of the career of taste as a phenomenon of the escape into unindictability. The interpretation of the genesis of the esthetic, which is sketched here, is to be seen in the context of points of view presented by J. Ritter in his lectures on esthetics in Münster from 1948 onward; cf. also O. Marquard, "Kant und die Wende zur Ästhetik," *Zeitschrift für philosophische Forschung*, 16 (1962) pp. 231–43 and 363–74. As a supplement to Ritter's thesis, this interpretation is at the same time an attempt to apply to the eighteenth century the macrothesis, which I am currently trying to develop, that esthetics and esthetic art emerge as compensation for "eschatological world-loss."
39. Bill of Rights in the Constitution of Virginia, 1776; Bill of Rights in the Constitution of the United States, and Déclaration des droits de l'homme et du citoyen en France; see M. Kriele, *Einführung in die Staatslehre* (Reinbek bei Hamburg, 1975), esp. pp. 149ff. What is most important to me here is that the fundamental and human rights do not institutionalize a compulsion to become "man in general," but rather a license to remain (in each case) this "particular man." The interpretive problems that emerge in this context cannot be pursued here.
40. Cf. F. W. J. Schelling, *Immanuel Kant* (1804), in *Sämmtliche Werke*, vol. 6

(1860), esp. pp. 4ff.; G. W. F. Hegel, *Vorlesungen über die Geschichte der Philosophie* (from 1816 onward), in *Werke in 20 Bänden*, E. Moldenhauer and K. M. Michel, eds., vol. 20 (Frankfurt, 1971), pp. 314 and 331–32; *Vorlesungen über die Philosophie der Geschichte* (from 1822 onward), ibid., vol. 11 (1970), pp. 525ff. Cf. H. Heine, *Zur Geschichte der Religion und Philosophie in Deutschland* (1834), in *Sämtliche Werke*, E. Elster, ed., vol. 4 (Leipzig/Vienna, 1890), esp. pp. 245ff., or *Religion and Philosophy in Germany: a fragment* (Albany, N.Y., 1986), pp. 101ff.

41. "The science of knowledge should be a pragmatic history of the human spirit" (J. G. Fichte, *Grundlage der Gesamten Wissenschaftslehre* [1794], in *Sämmtliche Werke*, vol. 1, p. 222).

42. See O. Marquard, "Schwierigkeiten mit der Geschichtsphilosophie," esp. pp. 14ff., 73ff.; idem, "Competence in Compensating for Incompetence?" in this volume; idem, "Exile der Heiterkeit," in W. Preisendanz and R. Warning, eds., *Das Komische* (Munich, 1976), esp. pp. 138ff.

43. H. Plessner, *Die verspätete Nation. Über die politische Verführbarkeit bürgerlichen Geistes* (1935) (Frankfurt a.M., 1974), p. 6.

44. G. Lukács, *Die Zerstörung der Vernunft* (1954) (Berlin, 1955), p. 6, or *The Destruction of Reason* (London: Merlin Press, 1962), p. 5: "There is no 'innocent' *weltanschauung*"; the context shows that what is meant is philosophy.

45. Cf. N. Hinske, "Die Geliebte mit den vielen Gesichtern," in H. Lübbe, ed., *Wozu Philosophie? Stellungnahmen eines Arbeitskreises* (Berlin/New York, 1978), esp. pp. 322ff.; cf. Plessner, *Die verspätete Nation*, esp. pp. 144ff.

46. Plessner, *Die verspätete Nation*, pp. 119ff.

47. See O. Marquard, "Skeptische Betrachtungen zur Lage der Philosophie," in H. Lübbe, *Wozu Philosophie?*, esp. pp. 84–87.

Translator's Note

a. This paper was presented to the German Society for the Study of the Eighteenth Century, in a conference at the Herzog August Library in Wolfenbüttel on Nov. 23, 1978.

=4=

The End of Fate?
(Some Observations on the Inevitability of Things Over Which We Have No Power of Disposition)

We live in the age in which things are makeable. At first nothing was made, then some things were made, and today everything is made.

Where things are made, things are thrown away. We live, at the same time, in the age of throwing away. At first nothing was thrown away, then some things were thrown away, and today everything is thrown away. We have the nonreturnable bottle, the nonreturnable bag—nonreturnable packaging in general—nonreturnable contents, nonreturnable things, a nonreturnable world. In what follows I attempt—as I have also attempted elsewhere—to conceive a nonreturnable thought. A nonreturnable thought is one that is thought and used only once and then never makes another appearance.[1] In conceiving this thought I proceed in a step by step manner, and my considerations are divided, by these steps, into sections. There are five such sections, and they are as follows: (1) the end of fate: God; (2) the end of God: the human compulsion to make things; (3) fate incognito: our lack of disposition over what is pregiven; (4) fate incognito: our lack of disposition over consequences; (5) beginning of a bad end. So much on the subject of organization; now let's get down to business.

The End of Fate: God

Habent su fata fata: the fates themselves have their fates. For first, as *moira, ananke,* and (with qualifications) as *nemesis, daimon, tyche,* and later as *heimarmene* and *fatum,* they were officially and explicitly fate; but then, it seems, they were not any longer: the way leads from *fatum* to *factum* (from fate to fact), from fatedness to madeness (*vom Schicksal zum Machsal*).

Schicksal—the German word[2] is a late one, apparently originating in the seventeenth century—and its Latin and Greek forerunner words[3] are words for what is inevitably necessary, ordained, decreed: for that, precisely, which one cannot choose, make, and make different, but which overpowers one, ties one down, and affects one willy-nilly. This is not only what is unexpected and sudden—the "blow of fate"—but also precisely what is allotted, imposed on, and apportioned to each particular life: its lot, its portion in life. *Moira* is connected to *meros,* part; no one lives to see everything, if only because everyone dies. It seems, too, that every fate is different; but there are fates that everyone experiences—for example, birth and death. Fate unites and fate isolates. There are collective fates: the flood in which everyone drowns. There are individual fates: the flood that Noah survives. Fates mark persons out: in the extreme case, by an individual's (external or internal) disfigurement, which condemns him or her to solitude; or even by the disfigurement of a whole lineage. An example is the curse of the house of Atreus, or—not to speak with unswerving seriousness here—the fate of a family in which, as an absentminded academic determined, childlessness was a hereditary characteristic for generations.

Fates mark persons out, or, to put it in up-to-date language, they establish identities; and they do this even where it is not a matter of exceptionally fortunate success or of very great misfortune. For the rest, one must seize one's fate, otherwise it might not "stick"—*fatum* requires *virtus.*[4] One must see "how merit and good fortune are linked,"[5] and guilt and misfortune. But merit and guilt may themselves be good fortune and misfortune, and therefore fate. Here too (and this

is the case absolutely everywhere in the context of fate) it is a matter of
the predetermined necessity—the unmakeable and unalterable quality,
beyond anyone's power of disposition—of what each person is and
what happens to them.

All of this, roughly speaking, is fate; but all of this is also, it seems,
in the past. Fate is no longer "up to date"; it is antiquated: a subject
for waves of nostalgia and for symposia funded by foundations. Nowadays each of us lives our own life, as a competent [*mündig*] individual:
the man is his own man, the woman is her own woman, the child is its
own child (and it is this even prenatally, if it is to have a properly
antiauthoritarian upbringing). The circumstances are shaped and produced by human self-determination, and fate, it seems, no longer carries any weight against this. This is the modern emancipation from
fate: "Men," Marx writes,[6] "make their own history"; the historical
world (so an early Fichtean, namely, Novalis,[7] formulates it) is a
"handwork." That becomes more palpably evident in our times; we
live in a world of present and future artifacts: what is, is made; what
has not yet been made, is already (or will soon be) makeable. Things
over which we have no power of disposition—things that no making
can reach—no longer exist; the unalterable, it seems, is played out;
fate has come to an end. This also affects the modern substitute versions of fate; they seem to lose their capacity to provoke an argument,
pro or contra. No one seems to get excited about determinism any
longer. Spengler's distinction between "the principle of causality and
the idea of fate"[8] is, it seems, an obsolete subtlety and no longer worth
the trouble. "Jensenism"[9] in the psychology of education seems—and I
emphasize: seems—to be a position that arrived after its time. And
Szondi's *Schicksalsanalyse* (analysis of fate)[10] was, at best, a rearguard
action. We no longer have anything to say about fate, unless (with or
without *Vorstudien zur Sabotage des Schicksals* [Preliminary studies
on the sabotage of fate])[11]—it is this, that we make it ourselves. Because the dominant view—dominant in the sense that those who oppose it seem a priori to have the burden of proof and a presumption of
moral questionableness or unacceptability against them—the dominant view is this: everything can be made, everything is at our disposal,
everything can and must be changed, and change is always improve-

ment. The emancipatory philosophy of history proclaims this for the big picture, and psychoanalysis discovers it—with an eye to both individuals and groups—in fine detail. Thomas Mann—yes, also Mann; even Mann—reminds us, in his second finest address about Freud, of Freud's formulation according to which "the giver of all the 'givens' resides in us, ourselves," and quotes a line from Jung, which "unmasks what 'befalls us' as what we 'make.' "[12] Even what supposedly only befalls us is a masked self-made thing, a disguised artifact. Fate is something made unconsciously.

Here—it seems—the claim of the concept of fate (and its variants) to recognition as a serious category of reality is shattered. At most, in places where no progressive tidying-up has been done, some fragments of fate still lie around to stumble over; in some cases with the appeal of curiosities: the "tricks of objects" and the "attractive power of what is referred to";[13] in some cases with a suggestion of contemporary wickedness or modishness: as "belief in fate" or "sworn sharing of fates," or as what is currently stylish (*schick*), à la mode, in whichever *Schickeria* ("trend-setting" group) it may be, all the way to "radical chic."[14, a] Overall, however, one can say: the triumphal progress of changeability and of making defatalizes reality.

Consequently fate also emigrates into the preserve called art. It becomes a category for the esthetics of tragedy.[15] *Wallenstein* is fertile in this respect: *In deiner Brust sind deines Schicksals Sterne* (the stars of your fate are in your breast).[16] A little later there are the plays about fatal dates, and the *Ahnfrau* ("The foremother," by Franz Grillparzer, 1817): the so-called tragedies of fate. Or fate presents itself in lyrical form: *So musst du sein, dir kannst du nicht entfliehn* (it is thus that you must be, you cannot escape yourself): Goethe, *Urworte, Orphisch* (First and last words: orphic);[17] or Hölderlin, *An die Parzen, Hyperions Schicksalslied* (To the fates; Hyperion's song of fate); but also Ferdinand Raimund: *Das Schicksal setzt den Hobel an und hobelt alle gleich* (fate applies the plane and planes everyone even).[18] Or it makes quasi-musical appearances: "Thus fate knocks on the door," a formulation that in the meantime has acquired a gamey flavor: and from the symphony of fate we then proceed to the opera—*Die Macht des Schicksals* (The power of fate)—and operetta: *Die Liebe, die Liebe ist eine Schicksalsmacht* (Love, love is a fatal power). I know I have that wrong; love, of course, is *eine Himmelsmacht* (a celestial power); but whatever Strauss and the *Zigeunerbaron* (gypsy baron) may say, *Schicksalsmacht* would also fit, and not only rhythmically. For fate finally becomes particularly suited to hit songs. No purveyor of hits can get by without fate: *Love Story* requires the "fate melody," and:

> *Ein Mann kehrt heim.* . . .
> *Er hat den Sternen sein Schicksal erzählt.* . . .
> *Er stand am Abgrund der Zeit.* . . .
> *Glück und Leid hielt sein Schicksal für ihn bereit.*
> (A man comes home. . . .
> He has told his fate to the stars. . . .
> He stood at the edge of the abyss of time. . . .
> His fate holds happiness and suffering in store for him.)

So Freddy[19] sings, on Polydor records, for those who believe, nowadays, in the starlets rather than the stars. That is a rich and interesting topic: *heimarmene* from Zeno to Heino. Taking it all together—even if these have only been indications, and the correctness of what I want to say is open to dispute—what it is will be evident: that from defatalized reality, which officially becomes the realm of making, fate flees into the realm of the esthetic, into the realm of the banal and the trivial, and finally into the realm of the banally and trivially esthetic: into the production of ready-made daydreams.

This history of the depletion of the power of fate, which ends thus, begins—if I see it correctly—with the antifatalism of Christianity. When the early church fathers write[20] *contra fatum* and *contra mathematicos*—that is, against the astrologers, the learned predictors of fate—the problem in the foreground is that of the freedom of the will: the fathers protest against fate as an excuse in ethical matters. But the truly central problem is this: fate is the rival of God's omnipotence. We Christians, Tatian writes, εἱμαρμένης ἐσμὲν ἀνώτεροι, (we are raised above *heimarmene*), and know, instead of the straying stars (*Irrsterne*, comets), only the one Lord, who never strays":[21] the almighty God. No sparrow falls if God does not want it to. For God is, at the same time, beyond all the details, the omnipotent and omni-

scient controller, because God is the absolute answer to the absolute
initial question: Why is there anything at all, instead of nothing? That
which is distinct from God—which, being contingent, cannot exist on
its own account—exists because God wants it to: because God begins
it and makes it from nothing—that is, creates it, and maintains it *per
concursum Dei et per creationem continuam* (by God's concurrence
and by continual creation). What had previously been the impotent
question directed at fate—Why did just this happen to me, to us, to
him, to her, to them?—the question of (as it is now called) "mastering
contingency"[22]—is surpassed in biblical Christianity and theological
metaphysics by the absolute initial question, to which God is the absolute answer: the omnipotent creator alone, and no one else, makes
everything and guides everything. This appeal to God—to creaturely
contingency and divine omnipotence—brings the career of fate to an
end: the one omnipotent God is the end of fate. And the modern
world, it seems, merely implements this end of fate, which in essence
was already accomplished earlier.

The End of God:
The Human Compulsion to Make Things

God—the God of the Bible, of Abraham, Isaac, and Jacob, who became the God of the philosophers and scholars—is the end of fate. If
that is the case, what does the end of God entail?

The end of God: with this formulation I cite an impression that
seems to be largely constitutive for the modern world and its tendency
toward making. With such constitutive phenomena it is not good to
rely on one's own experience. It is too solitary. For that reason, I
appeal here to others: to a philologist, two theologians, a sociologist, a
metaphysician and then, as a group, to other philosophers as well.

The philologist is Nietzsche. His formulation is famous: "God is
dead."[23] The cause of God's death, in Nietzsche's opinion, was God's
compassion. There is compassion only where there is suffering: the
evils in the world. *Si Deus, unde malum?* (If God exists, whence comes
evil?) It is this question—the question of God's compassion: the question of theodicy, addressed by God to God—that killed God. For: *Si*

malum, unde Deus? Where there are evils, God can only be justified—
even to God—by God's nonexistence; which is to say, by God's death.
The continuance and the growth of evils—the miscarriage of creation
and of redemption—require the end of God, or at any rate (but this
comes to the same thing) the end of God's omnipotence.

This—fundamentally and precisely this—is also said, in their own
way, by two theologians: the early Habermas and the later Oeing-
Hanhoff. Oeing-Hanhoff (who was just belated) formulates it in a
systematic and direct form, when—in search of a theodicy—he asserts
"that [God] can renounce omnipotence," or, which is the same thing,
"[can renounce] divinity, in favor of finite freedom,"[24] and does renounce it. In this way freedom for making and for wickedness becomes possible for those who are not God: for human beings. Early
Habermas produces the same formulation as an interpretation of
Schelling's philosophy of the ages of the world. In view of the corrup-
tion of creation, Schelling's "idea of a contraction of God" (which is
part of his philosophy of the ages of the world) promises, in Habermas's opinion, a theodicy: we arrive at a "world that has slipped out
of God's hands, and whose history has been turned over" thereby to
"the 'inverted God' of humankind in society," as a result (Habermas
says Schelling says) of "God's withdrawal into himself" and "into the
past."[25] By this withdrawal God turns history over to human freedom:
God's resignation makes God into, as it were, the initiator of Left
Hegelianism and the indirect protector even of Critical Theory.

The same opinion is held, it seems to me, by a Germanistic/
theological sociologist—namely, Dorothee Sölle. With an "atheistic
faith in God," her "theology after the death of God" deals with God's
retreat: it deals with the "God who is powerless in the world," who
"needs help," first of all from Christ, who deputizes for the "absent
God," and then from humans, who, as deputies of this "deputy," act—
this is, indeed, the conclusion—in the place of God.[26] God's death
compels human beings to make their things themselves.

That—and now I cite a metaphysician who does not want to be a
metaphysician—is Heidegger translated into the language of theology.
When Being (and "Being" is a pseudonym for God) withdraws, in the
"history of Being," it turns the world over, itself, to the metaphysical

logic of objectification, to the will to power, to technique. When Being—and with it (compare Heidegger's Hölderlin interpretations on this score) Christ, as the last of the gods—makes its exit, humans are empowered to make things.[27]

It is evident that the persons I have cited here do not only say similar things; they say the same thing. At any rate it is possible to think this when one notes that at bottom it makes no difference whether God's resignation is thought of as an interim or as a definitive state, and that it is a less important nuance whether God is disempowered or God's existence is negated. It is also of secondary importance, in that connection, whether this is done by humans or by God: whether, that is, in line with an antitheological atheism, humans no longer believe in God, or whether, in line with a theological atheism, God no longer believes in God and consequently retires and dies. It amounts to the same thing— which is a fact that I have to underline. For the persons I quoted together here (with misleading labels that tell the truth) cannot, in fact, desire to be quoted together. For that very reason, the agreement that they pains- takingly disguise is an exceptionally impressive piece of evidence for the fact that what is in question here is a converging tendency in the modern history of philosophy, or in the modern self-understanding: a tendency that should not be surprising. For the power of human freedom is made possible by God's powerlessness. The fact that humankind, in modern times, becomes maker, creator, and redeemer, is due precisely to the fact that God ceases to be these things. Human autonomy is made possible by the depletion of God's power. Intentionally or not, or with differing degrees of explicitness, this was emphasized first of all by German Idealism (the idealism that runs from Kant to Marx, and whose radical position is represented, in my opinion, by Fichte), with its inference from God's goodness to God's nonexistence: human beings must (con- sciously or unconsciously) make reality themselves, because God is good and—in view of the evils, antinomies, antagonisms—can remain good only by not existing. That is the theodicy that works through an atheism *ad maiorem Dei gloriam* (to the greater glory of God).[28] It is what the persons I have quoted here all, in principle, advocate—namely, a theology of the *Deus emeritus* (retired God).

It is, nota bene, worth pondering the fact that what stood at the beginning of this depletion of God's power was the extreme theology of omnipotence that marked the late Middle Ages. The path from the theology of the *potentia absoluta* (absolute power) by way of the theology of the *Deus absconditus* and the *Dieu caché* (hidden God) and the theology of the *Deus emeritus* to theology after the death of God—is a remarkable sequence. Perhaps even omnipotence was already powerlessness by other means. But this is offered only as an incidental observation. For what I wanted to do here, overall, was only to point to what is going on in philosophy when (in a way that is constitutive of modernity) the issue is what I have called "the end of God."

I repeat my question. God is the end of fate. If that is the case, what does the end of God mean? Does fate return once again, in a posttheistic, modern guise? To be sure, the opposite seems to be the case. Look at the artificial world in which we live, and at its self-understanding, which I sketched at the outset. But is it true that in the contemporary world, as a result of the modified "omnipotence of making" that humankind inherited from God, fate is definitively conquered and at an end? Or does this only seem to be the case? Is it possible that the official and manifest tendency toward human omnipotence of making is counteracted by a latent and unofficial tendency: an indirect reempowerment of fate? It is time to formulate and to test this undoubtedly risky thesis. In modern times, after the end of the God who was the end of fate, the official defatalization of the world is accompanied by its unofficial refatalization; or, putting it differently, the outcome of the modern disempowerment of divine omnipotence is not only the official triumph of human freedom but also the unofficial return of fate.

In the two following sections I should like to draw attention to two things that could help to give this thesis a certain degree of plausibility.

Fate Incognito:
Our Lack of Disposition over Prior Givens

First is the fact, unavoidable for human beings, of their lack of disposition over what is pregiven. This fact—it seems; and this is, on the face of it, paradoxical—becomes inescapable precisely in modern times;

and it can be interpreted as a return (in, admittedly, an altered and pseudonymous form) of fate. I should like to explain this briefly.

For human beings it is a difficult task, after the death of God, to remain human. In the first place, as soon as God's position becomes vacant they feel compelled to be a candidate for it. That is, of course, the reason why from now on they have the task, which was previously God's affair, of making everything. When they nevertheless resist this pressure for promotion to the role of the absolute, humans encounter (in modern times) the problem of saving their finitude in a situation in which the theological definition of their finitude—the status of being a "creature"—is increasingly no longer available. Here the attempt to define their finitude emphatically as mortality enters the breach: in existential philosophy, as "Being toward death," and in (philosophical) anthropology as being "unburdened" (always only for a certain period) of (the likelihood of imminent) death.[29] *Vita brevis* (life is short): this applies—think of the time pressure resulting from the need to provide against contingencies—down to the level of detail, as well, then; which is precisely why saving time is—in spite of the danger of ennui—a *bonum evidentissimum* (most manifest good).

But important though it is, the equation "finitude is mortality" is not sufficient. It only implies, but does not make explicit, the other aspect, which is at least equally important: that human beings never begin at the beginning. Their life is an interim: where it ceases, it is at an end, but where it begins is never the beginning. For reality— forestalling them—is always already there, and they have to link up with it. No human is an absolute beginning: they all live with prior givens over which they have no power of disposition. Consequently there is also a legitimacy of the things that are nearest at hand, as opposed to the first things, and there is a modern ritual of modesty that demonstrates this noninitial, postliving status of human beings— the way they are inevitably referred to prior givens over which they have no power of disposition. This is the warding off, by the critique of metaphysics, of the question of the absolute beginning. One who asks about the beginning wants to be the beginning; and one who wants to be the beginning does not want to be a human being, but the absolute. Consequently humans in modern times take leave—in favor of their humanity (when they refuse to become the absolute)—of first principles, of the ἀρχή (beginning, principle), and they wager, then, on conceptions that make superfluous, that suspend the question of the absolute beginning—the question of absolute justification.

Hans Blumenberg[30] has interpreted the modern idea of self-preservation as such a theorem of suspension. Because self-preservation implies the superfluousness of preservation by something else, through creation, there is thenceforth a (refutable) presumption in favor of the adequate justification of what exists: *conservatione sui* (by self-preservation) it is and remains what it is, if it is not altered by discoverable causes; so one no longer has to explain why it exists, but only why it becomes different—in case it becomes different. That, says Blumenberg, is "a kind of rule of the burden of proof." It reduces the burdens of giving reasons to finite—which is to say, to humanly manageable—dimensions, by laying it down that the burden of giving reasons, the burden of proof, goes with alteration.

Linking up with the English jurists' tradition of the "common law," Martin Kriele has shown that this holds not only where one wants to comprehend changes, theoretically, but also where one wants to bring about changes, practically.[31] There, too, it is reasonable initially and refutably—and I emphasize: refutably—to presume the adequacy of what exists. The burden of proof is on the advocate of change.

Niklas Luhmann calls this the "involuntary conservatism produced by complexity."[32] It is unavoidable because, given finite capacity, not everything can be up for disposition at once, but always only specific things, in relation to specific alternatives, which bear the burden of proof. To proceed otherwise would be so complicated that our finite capacity of comprehension, which requires the reduction of complexity, could not keep up. This is why, in Luhmann's opinion, there is a compelling need to "accept history as a basis for action."

Formulated in the precise language of systems theory, that is exactly the fundamental idea of the hermeneutic approach in modern philosophy. Only if what is historically present is "always already" there, without our doing anything about it, as a prior given, does what we do contribute have a chance. No man can begin absolutely from the beginning; everyone has to link up ("hypoleptically," as Joachim Ritter says[33]) with what is already there: a future (*Zukunft*) has to have a derivation (*Herkunft*). This hermeneutic insight promotes and trains the *amor fati* (love of fate) to be the "child of its time": *Hic Rhodus, hic saltus* (here is Rhodes, make your jump here).[34] And the jumps that one can make there are not, in fact, great ones. The latitude that is available is determined by what is already present, as a *fait accompli* (accomplished fact): as a *fait* not only in the sense of the minifate that we call a "datum," but also in the sense of the maxifate that we call a "*fatum*" (destiny, fate). At the same time one has to see that this is not a devastating limitation, but is, rather, precisely a vital opportunity for human beings. Because they are not the absolute, they need this quantity to link up with; without it they could not live, let alone change anything.

All this can also be formulated as follows. Precisely on account of their noninitial position—their "hypoleptic" mode of life—humans have an inescapable need for fatalism. And this is not only true, for example, of opportunists, who expect to benefit from the way events take their course, or of defeatists, who prefer certain defeat to an uncertain outcome. Because those who want to act in certain realms have to rely on the fact that they do not have to act in others—which are always the greater number. In this sense, their activity depends on their inactivity, and their making depends on the fact that they do not, in fact, make most things, but—*sit venia verbo* (if the expression is permitted)—they accept them as fate. Thus everyone who does not want to be a fatalist requires a great deal of fatalism. The fact that one does not have to make everything, or, putting it differently, that most things are and have been "always already" taking their course, without one's having to do anything—this fate, this destiny, is the condition of the possibility of action that extends as far as human action can.

This (in my opinion, reasonable) fatalism, together with its agents, such as the "institutions,"[b] reduces burdens of action to the dimensions of the human capacity for action: it brings what has to be done within the range of the talents of human actors. Human praxis always does (or "makes": *macht*) only the little that still remains to be done; for it to be possible, there must already be, to a very considerable extent, "nothing more to be done." That is, at the same time, the reason why—even after saying farewell to the *scientia non humana sed divina* (not human but divine science): to metaphysics—persons continue to be disposed, precisely in the *scientia humana*, the "humanities," toward theory. Because theory is what one does when there is nothing else whatever to be done.

On the whole, then, the situation seems to be this: in modern times—after the end of God—there is a relationship of conditionality between fatalism and humanity; in that situation, the attempt of human beings to save their humanity, against every expectation that they should become God, requires the reempowerment of fate. That was the first of the two things to which I wanted to draw attention.

Fate Incognito:
Our Lack of Disposition over Consequences

Second is the fact, unavoidable for human beings, that they do not have disposition over consequences. This too—it seems; and this is, on the face of it, paradoxical—becomes inescapable precisely in modern times. And it too, and it in particular, can be interpreted as a return (in, admittedly, an altered and pseudonymous form) of fate. I should like to explain this, too, briefly.

For humankind, as I said, it is a difficult task, after the end of God, to remain human. For as soon as God's position becomes vacant, they feel compelled to become candidates for it. That is, I repeat, why from now on they have the task, which was previously God's affair, of making everything. Persons take up this inherited task emphatically when they yield to the pressure to become the absolute, in order to avoid the fatalism that I have sketched. On that account they become—and a representative instance of this in the history of philosophy is, it seems to me, the step from Kant to Fichte: the step into the end of modesty, out of the modern age into the countermodern age—the absolute. But how is that: Can human beings be the absolute? For absolute emancipation into the status of the absolute, the classical answer is: they can, because they should; or, in contemporary jargon, they have a "counterfactual competence." Anything else is a lazy Kantian or a wishy-washy positivist excuse. Thus—neoabsolutistically—the farewell to first principles is retracted, and the question of the absolute beginning is set up again. Why—so it runs in its modern form, as the question of absolute legitimation—that is, by what right, is there anything, rather than nothing at all, apart from myself? The human being who asks for the absolute beginning becomes by this question, the absolute beginning—that is, the absolute "super-ego" (*Über-Ich*) of reality as a whole.

In the meantime—in the age of communication, and not only of bilateral/dialogical but also of multilateral/interactionist communication—this "I" has turned into a "we": into the absolute communication community, the absolute "super-we." Nothing is allowed to oppose it, everything is supposed to be "for it"; and what is for it is, in doubtful cases, only its creatures. Thus everything has to become its creature, through the counterfactual creative competence of this "we": through absolute social making. Therefore everything was and is made—according to neoabsolutism—by human beings.

But because it is after all, factually, human, this counterfactually absolute making in fact lacks omnipotence; and consequently it brings about things that it does not intend. The consequences, even indirect consequences, escape its control; they get outside its power of disposition. The reasons why this is the case can be specified, for example, sociologically. Friedrich H. Tenbruck has tried to do this.[35] Realities (social realities, for example, institutions) that are done away with, by an act of intervention, on account of manifest failure or offense, have (as a rule) latent functions, the nonperformance of which causes mischief. And to the extent that achievements brought about by successful changes become matters of course, their capacity to satisfy tends toward zero. This surprises not only the practical makers—who, after all, make their plans in a situation where something is lacking, and therefore necessarily overestimate the capacity of their success to satisfy—but also the theoretical despisers of constants, in the "critical" school, which they uncritically regard as constant the capacity of such accomplishments to gratify. Of course the dialecticians (and above all those who live for the revolution and by its nonarrival) hardly ever count on being overtaken by what they always think about in relation to the others and seldom in relation to themselves—namely, the dialectic. So it is not, for example, only unsuccessful planned making, but precisely the successful kind, that plans itself (at least partially) out of its success. Consequently, in the age of the fate-abolishing zeal of human beings for making, things that were well-intended do not turn out well. Absolute disposition over things establishes things over which we have no disposition. Outcomes compromise intentions; absolute world amelioration miscarries and becomes world confusion.

Since the French Revolution and up to the present, these are the great disillusioning lessons of human self-making, when persons promote themselves, in the modern manner, to the position of commissarial God. These lessons are due to our lack of disposition over consequences. Consequently, simultaneously with the progress of making and its orders of magnitude, we have to develop techniques for living with these disillusionments. But these very techniques, it seems to me, reactivate fate.

The issue is techniques for dealing with disillusionment. Of course the first thing one tries is to avoid disillusionment by means of the art of ignoring. Thus, currently, for example, memory—the sense of history—is disparaged. Comparisons between what was brought about and what was there before are not to take place. But apparently that is not enough; one has to have recourse to stronger remedies. Thus we arrive at the large-scale cultivation of excuses, a boom in exculpatory arrangements, an exorbitant need for scapegoats; in short, at the art of not having been responsible. A favorite multipurpose alibi is society; that is, *other* persons. For when things go wrong, it is true that (in modern times) it is human beings—makers—who were responsible, but always only the other human beings: to exculpate oneself and explain the quality gradient between what was aimed at and what actually takes place, one needs the figure of the antagonist, who, as *diabolus redivivus* (the devil reborn), betrays and thwarts the blessings of progress. This compulsion to feel impeded and betrayed, which Manès Sperber calls "the police conception of history,"[36] serves to shift the responsibility to the neofates or Norns who are on call and who are defined in terms no longer taken from the textile sector, as spinners of the threads of fate, but rather from the metal sector, as wire-pullers. By accusing them, the world-creating "super-we" puts its disappointments with its creation behind it; as it were, the "we" posits itself by disengaging itself from the "not we": in the extreme case, from enemies, to whom the fault for the failure of the autonomous making is ascribed. Evidently human beings who promote themselves to the position of the absolute fall under this compulsion to separate others from themselves and turn them into enemies. Their tendency then is no longer to act humanly, as human beings, but only absolutely, as the enemies of enemies; the neoabsolute philosophy of self-making is, it seems, not only theology after the end of God but also anthropology after the end of humanity.

This, then, is the way it runs: the human absolute intention of being absolutely responsible develops into the art of not having been responsible—that is, into the art of making others responsible. That is an indirect empowerment of fate: the more that humans make reality themselves, the more they finally, disillusioned, declare it to be something they cannot do anything about and which now is only inflicted on them. Modern neoabsolute and emancipatory antifatalism evidently tends to become its opposite: fatalism; its defatalization of the world indirectly promotes refatalization.

At the same time we hear—and this confirms the finding I just stated—a direct call for a great necessity: for a necessary turning toward the good, which catches up with, overcomes, outwits, and (at least in the long run) compensates for the unpleasant consequences of making. Precisely where humans, in the modern manner, make their own history, they seek a superhuman guarantee that whatever they may produce, in their blissful making, and however unpleasant things may become as a result, the historical outcome will be better and, ultimately, will be the good. An interest arises in history's having a necessary—which is to say, a fatalistic—course. Of course, "I feel as though I were annihilated" (Georg Büchner writes) "by the monstrous fatalism of history."[37] When confidence in the necessity of the course of history can, in this way, turn into distrust and desperation, one needs additional guarantees, from the beginning, of its taking a good course. They are postulated: first of all God, then nature, and finally the world-spirit and other protagonists down to the proletariat and the elites of antielitism. In the language of transcendental philosophy, they all belong to the doctrine of postulates: one has to believe in them, because the only alternative is to believe in them.[38] They are meant to oppose "fatal" consequences of making, as a counter-fate.

In the meantime, these postulates have been brought from the transcendental Beyond into historical immanence and given permanent appointments: as augurs of the dictates of reality. They make up the planning staffs of the bureaucracies of progress in the administered world; and they are—this has to be appreciated—postulates that have become intraworldly. What they lose, in the form of the aura of the Beyond, they gain in an immanent aura, in that (where the realization that good advice is expensive has led persons to the conclusion that expensive advice is good) these postulates are no longer just postulated, now, but—the better to impress us—are paid as well: by the assignment, to them, of power, honor, and money. They are responsible for the necessities to which the autonomously produced unpleasant consequences compel us, necessities that force the course of the world—the course that was supposedly under control—to "flee forward." Such necessities are formulated (with complicated calculations) and ordained by the great plans: the overall plan is horoscope and fate in one.

I have always been impressed by the fairy tales in which fairies step up to various cradles in order to pronounce their wishes (for the babies); these were evidently members of planning staffs in the days when wishing still made a difference. The penultimate fairy is always the wicked one; she contributes the curses. Nowadays she is superfluous. In one of the unusual cases where a reduction has taken place in the division of labor, the curses are now developed immediately as part of the well-intended planning projects, because the opposite of good is good intentions; and all planning projects nowadays are well-intended. The inventors of those fairy tales had, I think, a very good sense of how things work in reality; because the last fairy, the good one, could never make it as though the curses had not been pronounced; the only help she could provide was a compensating wish that worked in the opposite direction. So this last fairy was the compensation fairy.

The compensation occupation nowadays—the crisis management practiced by planners and makers—also has to work in the opposite direction: it tries to produce measures against the consequences that have gotten out of control; but in doing so—the good and the bad fairies being strictly identical here—it again immediately produces consequences that get out of control, and (if I see the matter correctly) it does this all the more, the less (on account of the euphoria of omnipotence) it carries out the hypoleptic duties of linking up with prior natural and historical givens. When, through the workings of the compulsion to "flee forward," the future becomes reckless toward the past from which it derives, the compensating plans become, at best, scrap paper; they then project futures that will never come, and are thus, in a new way, museumlike: a futurologist is an antiquarian turned so he faces forward. But in the worst case the plans and interventions become involuntary accomplices in putting the course of the world beyond our disposition. Then precisely the attempts at dominating it, which have the greatest zeal for making, operate to promote its "fatal" quality: in the extreme case, by implementing the law of the conservation of absurdity. In that case, a minimum level of confusion is continually reestablished, and when it is interrupted by efforts to create order, this interruption is immediately eliminated again, by, precisely, the efforts to create order. Anyone who considers the planning agencies—for example, those responsible for educational planning—really has to come to the conclusion that this is the more likely course of events.

Planning is, at least frequently, a continuation of chaos by other means. That is the cunning of unreason: humankind's omnipotence to make things reempowers what they have no disposition over: destiny; their autonomous antifatalism reveals itself as antiautonomous fatalism; their banishing of fate (in their intoxication with "making") recalls it, in practice. And just where humans—officially—become the heirs of its absolute end, fate is—unofficially—inescapably there again.

Beginning of a Bad End

Those were only two remarks meant to elucidate a risky global thesis that I had formulated as follows: in modern times, after the end of the God who was the end of fate, the official defatalization of the world is accompanied by its unofficial refatalization; or, putting it differently, the outcome of the modern disempowerment of divine omnipotence is not only the official triumph of human freedom but also the unofficial return of fate. I had a chance to suggest to what an extent this return of fate is at the same time the permanence of misfortunes—not, indeed, absolutely, but certainly in those cases where humans forget the duties to "link up" that go with their finite constitution, and instead occupy the position of counterfactual omnipotence. Just this—not, that is, the modern fatalism of humanly antiabsolute modesty, which I sketched in my first remark, but the antimodern fatalism that follows from the step into the antihuman immodesty of a human attempt at omnipotence (which I sketched in my second remark)—seems to be the dominant "trend." Consequently, one can harbor the fear that "it will end badly."[39]

One who ends his reflections on an indirect return of fate—badly—with the fear that it will end badly, has every reason to point out two circumstances that relativize this result. First: this series of lectures begins with my reflections, but—thank God—it does not end with them; and so the beginner of this series can direct the listeners' expectations away from himself, to those who do not speak first, as beginners, but only after the beginner, and are thus the advanced contributors. Secondly: on account of this beginning, with its bad end, I have to insist on the truth of what I said at the outset: my goal here was to conceive a nonreturnable thought, an impermanent thought that is immediately relieved again of its burdensome contents, because it instantly disappears; because (and I repeat) a nonreturnable thought is a thought that is thought and used only once and then never reappears—except perhaps, unfortunately, as a problem of environmental pollution. And this, I think, is precisely the situation here with this throwaway theory about the unsuccessful end and the indirect reempowerment of fate.

Notes

1. G. Patzig and C. Meier must take at least some of the blame for this formulation.
2. See the article "Schicksal," in *Deutsches Wörterbuch,* ed. J. and W. Grimm, vol. 8 (Leipzig, 1893), cols. 2659–60.
3. See especially the article "Heimarmene" by W. Gundel, in *Paulys Realencyclopädie der Classischen Altertumswissenschaft,* begun by G. Wissowa, vol. 7

(Stuttgart, 1912), cols. 2622–45; and the article "Fatum (Heimarmene)" by H. O. Schröder, in *Realencyclopädie für Antike und Christentum*, vol. 7 (Stuttgart, 1969), cols. 524–636.

4. See M. Landmann, "Virtus und Fatum," in his *Pluralität und Antinomie* (Munich/Basel, 1963), pp. 151–97, and "Eine Lanze für das Schicksal," in his *Das Ende des Individuums*. *Anthropologische Skizzen* (Stuttgart, 1971), pp. 208–14.

5. J. W. Goethe, *Faust II*, lines 5061–64, in *Werke*, Hamburg edition in 14 vols., vol. 3 (10th printing, Munich, 1976), p. 158.

6. K. Marx, *Der 18te Brumaire des Louis Napoleon* [The eighteenth Brumaire of Louis Napoleon], in K. Marx/F. Engels, *Werke*, vol. 8 (Berlin, 1960), p. 115.

7. Novalis, "Das allgemeine Brouillon" (1798/1799), in *Schriften. Die Werke Friedrich von Hardenbergs*, ed. P. Kluckhohn and R. Samuel, vol. 3 (2nd printing, Stuttgart, 1969), pp. 247–48.

8. O. Spengler, *Der Untergang des Abendlandes* [The decline of the West] (1918) (Munich, 1972), pp. 152ff.

9. See H. J. Eysenck, *Vererbung, Intelligenz und Erziehung. Zur Kritik der pädagogischen Milieutheorie* (Stuttgart, 1975), pp. 36ff. (original: *The IQ Argument: Race, Intelligence and Education* [New York, 1971]).

10. L. Szondi, *Schicksalsanalyse* (1944) (second ed., Basel, 1948).

11. U. Sonnemann, *Negative Anthropologie. Vorstudien zur Sabotage des Schicksals* (Hamburg, 1969).

12. Thomas Mann, "Freud und die Zukunft" (1936), in *Werke. Schriften und Reden zur Literatur, Kunst und Philosophie*, vol. 2 (Frankfurt a.M., 1960), pp. 222, 221; see also pp. 213–31 in toto.

13. Friedrich Theodor Vischer, *Auch Einer. Eine Reisebekanntschaft* (1879) (fifth printing, Stuttgart/Leipzig/Berlin/Vienna, 1891), p. 24 and many other places; W. von Scholz, *Der Zufall, eine Vorform des Schicksals* (*Die Anziehungskraft des Bezüglichen*) (Stuttgart, 1924).

14. T. Wolfe, *Radical Chic und Mau Mau bei der Wohlfahrtsbehörde* (Hamburg, 1972), esp. pp. 5ff. (original: *Radical Chic and Mau-Mauing the Flack Catchers* [New York, 1970]).

15. Representative instances: F. W. J. Schelling, "Philosophische Briefe über Dogmatismus und Kritizismus" (1795), in *Sämmtliche Werke*, ed. K. F. A. Schelling, part 1, vol. 1 (Stuttgart/Augsburg, 1857), esp. pp. 336–37, and "Philosophie der Kunst" (1802), same ed., part 1, vol. 5 (1860), pp. 693ff. See also same ed., part 1, vol. 5 (1860), pp. 429–30, and the "System des transzendentalen Idealismus" (1800), same ed., part 1, vol. 3 (1860), pp. 603–4. The historical period characterized by "fate," Schelling tells us, is the "tragic" period, and tragedy is the collision of freedom with fate, while "epic . . . does not involve fate" (vol. 5, p. 646). Hegel tells us, on the contrary, that "the dominant reality in the epic—and not, as one commonly hears, in drama—is . . .

fate" (*Vorlesungen über die Ästhetik* [1818, and subsequent years], in *Werke in 20 Bänden*, Theorie-Werkausgabe, ed. E. Moldenhauer and K. M. M. Michel, vol. 15 [Frankfurt am Main, 1970], p. 364). Compare (same ed.) pp. 521ff.: tragedy leaves fate behind it and establishes the ethical world. See, overall, B. von Wiese, *Die deutsche Tragödie von Lessing bis Hebbel* (1948) (eighth printing, Hamburg, 1961).

16. F. Schiller, "Die Piccolomini" (1799), II, 6; in *Sämtliche Werke,* centennial edition in 16 vols., vol. 5, ed. J. Minor (Stuttgart/Berlin, 1905), p. 105.

17. Goethe, *Werke,* Hamburg ed., vol. 1 (10th printing, Munich, 1974), p. 359.

18. F. Raimund, "Der Verschwender. Original-Zaubermärchen in drei Aufzügen" (1834), III, 6, in *Sämtliche Werke,* historical/critical centennial edition, ed. F. Brukner and E. Castle, vol. 2 (Vienna, 1934), pp. 434–35. On the theme of equality brought about by fate and equality of fates see, for example, P. H. Azaïs, *Des compensations dans les destinées humaines* (1808), vol. 1 (3rd printing, Paris, 1818), p. 29: "Le sort de l'homme, consideré dans son ensemble, est l'ouvrage de la nature entière, et tous les hommes sont égaux par leur sort."

19. [F. Quinn] "Ein Mann kehrt heim," text and music by P. Orloff, in *top Schlagertextheft,* no. 43 (Hamburg, n.d.), p. 12.

20. See the article "Fatum" in REAC (cited in note 3).

21. Tatian, *Oratio ad Graecos,* 9, 5. Here I have to pass over the fact that in the patristic tradition from, in fact, as early as Justin—see especially Augustine (for example, *De Civitate Dei,* 5,1ff.)—this disjunctive interpretation is sometimes weakened into a mediating one: God's omnipotent providence is then no longer the negation of fate, for the latter now counts as a distorted or figurative expression for divine providence. R. Guardini gives a modern version of this account in his *Freiheit, Gnade, Schicksal* (1948) (5th printing, Munich, 1967), esp. pp. 173ff.

22. See for example H. Lübbe, *Fortschritt als Orientierungsproblem* (Freiburg, 1975), esp. pp. 176ff.

23. F. Nietzsche in, for example, *Die fröhliche Wissenschaft* [The Gay Science] (1881/1882), in *Werke,* ed. K. Schlechta, vol. 2 (Munich, 1955), pp. 115, 126–28, 206; *Also sprach Zarathustra* [Thus Spake Zarathustra] (1883/1884), same vol., pp. 279, 280, 348 ("God died of His pity for men"), pp. 498, 501, 522–23.

24. L. Oeing-Hanhoff, "Mensch und Recht bei Thomas von Aquin," *Philosophisches Jahrbuch,* 82 (1975) 29; compare pp. 28–31.

25. J. Habermas, "Dialektischer Idealismus im Übergang zum Materialismus—Geschichtsphilosophische Folgerungen aus Schellings Idee einer Contraction Gottes" (1963), in his *Theorie und Praxis* (Frankfurt am Main, 1971), pp. 172–227, esp. pp. 190–93. Translated as *Theory and Practice* (Boston, 1973).

26. D. Sölle, *Stellvertretung. Ein Kapitel Theologie nach dem "Tode Gottes"* (Stuttgart/Berlin, 1965), esp. pp. 189–205; and idem, *Atheistisch an Gott glauben* (Olten, 1968), esp. pp. 68ff.

27. See especially M. Heidegger, "Die seinsgeschichtliche Bestimmung des Nihilismus" (1944–1946), in his *Nietzsche*, vol. 2 (Pfullingen, 1961), pp. 335–98, esp. p. 353 (*Nietzsche*, vol. 4, trans. F. A. Capuzzi [San Francisco, 1982], p. 214): "The matter stands . . . with the concealment of Being as such. Being itself stays away." p. 355 (trans. Capuzzi, p. 215): "Being itself withdraws." p. 383 (trans. Capuzzi, pp. 238–39): "The essential unfolding of nihilism is the default of Being as such. . . . Being keeps to itself with its own essence. . . . But when Being (*das Sein*) itself withdraws into its remotest withholding, the being (*das Seiende*) as such arises, released as the exclusive standard for 'Being,' into the totality of its dominion. Beings (*das Seiende*) as such appear as will to power." Compare W. Weischedel, *Der Gott der Philosophen*, vol. 1 (Darmstadt, 1972), esp. pp. 491–92.

28. See O. Marquard, "Idealismus und Theodizee" (1965), in his *Schwierigkeiten mit der Geschichtsphilosophie* (Frankfurt a.M., 1973), pp. 52–65.

29. M. Heidegger, *Sein und Zeit* (Halle, 1927), translated as *Being and Time* (New York, 1962). A. Gehlen, *Der Mensch. Seine Natur und seine Stellung in der Welt* (1940) (9th printing, Frankfurt a.M., 1971), translated as *Man, His Nature and Position in the World* (New York, 1988).

30. H. Blumenberg, *Selbsterhaltung und Beharrung. Zur Konstitution der neuzeitlichen Rationalität* (Wiesbaden, 1970); see esp. p. 39: "primarily as a proposition about the burden of proof."

31. M. Kriele, *Theorie der Rechtsgewinnung* (Berlin, 1967); summary statement on p. 312: "the presumptive binding force of precedent. There is a (refutable) presumption in favor of the reasonableness of all precedents." Compare M.K., *Die Herausforderung des Verfassungsstaats* (Neuwied/Berlin, 1970), esp. pp. 18–20.

32. N. Luhmann, "Status quo als Argument," in H. Baier, ed., *Studenten in Opposition. Beiträge zur Soziologie der deutschen Hochschule* (Bielefeld, 1968), pp. 73–82, esp. pp. 78, 81.

33. From the Greek ὑπόληψις, linking up with what the previous speaker said; see J. Ritter, *Metaphysik und Politik* (Frankfurt am Main, 1969), p. 64: The "hermeneutic method leads . . . to the path of hypoleptic linking up"; and p. 66: "hermeneutic hypolepsis." See the article "Hypolepsis" by G. Bien, in J. Ritter et al., eds., *Historisches Wörterbuch der Philosophie*, vol. 3 (Basel/Stuttgart, 1974), cols. 1252–54. Compare H.-G. Gadamer, *Wahrheit und Methode* (1960) (third printing, Tübingen, 1972), pp. 250–90; translated as *Truth and Method* (New York, 1975). The connection between Kriele's "presumptive force of precedents" and Gadamer's "rehabilitation of the concept of prejudice" (p. 261) needs to be looked into.

34. G. W. F. Hegel, *Grundlinien der Philosophie des Rechts* (1821), in *Werke* (cited in n. 15), vol. 7 (1970), p. 26.

35. F. H. Tenbruck, *Zur Kritik der planenden Vernunft* (Freiburg/Munich, 1972).

36. M. Sperber, *Die Achillesferse* (Frankfurt a.M./Hamburg, 1969), esp. pp. 75–76. Translated as *The Achilles Heel* (Garden City, N.Y., 1960).
37. G. Büchner, *Sämtliche Werke nebst Briefen und anderen Dokumenten*, ed. H. J. Meinerts (Darmstadt, 1963), p. 391.
38. "Postulates" in the sense given to the term by I. Kant, *Kritik der praktischen Vernunft* [Critique of practical reason] (1788), in *Gesammelte Schriften*, Academy edition, vol. 5 (Berlin, 1908), pp. 122ff.
39. This is the formulation of a character named Schwabing-Oblomow in May Spils (director), *Zur Sache, Schätzchen* (Frankfurt am Main: Nobis distributors, 1969). Compare F. Schiller, *Die Braut von Messina* (1803), I, 8, in *Sämtliche Werke*, centennial edition, vol. 7, (1905), p. 41: "Yes, it didn't begin well, believe me, and it doesn't end well."

Translator's Notes

a. The point of this punning sally depends upon the fact that "fate," in German, is *Schicksal*.
b. "Institution"—a technical term introduced, in this sense, by Arnold Gehlen in his *Urmensch und Spätkultur* (Bonn, 1956)—refers to habitual patterns of perception, behavior, and interaction which humankind has developed to take the place of instincts (with which it is poorly equipped), and as a stable background for its conscious initiatives.

= 5 =

In Praise of Polytheism
(On Monomythic and Polymythic Thinking)

My consciousness of the great honor that is done to me by the invitation to contribute to a colloquium on myth is combined with an intense fear and a timid hope. I am afraid that I was invited because it is supposed that I possess competence in the area of the philosophy of mythology. That would be an outright mistake, because I have none. I do, however, have something else—namely, the timid hope, just mentioned, that, quite to the contrary, those who invited me—knowing more about this incompetence of mine in the philosophy of mythology than I could wish—had one or even both of two very different reasons. The first would be this: I am allowed to speak not only despite, but precisely on account of my incompetence in the philosophy of mythology, because there is a desire, in this colloquium—let us say, in the interests of parity—to let a representative nonexpert have a say, with a paradigmatically incompetent statement. Only one nonexpert, it is true (after all, every rule of parity once started small), but at least one, nevertheless. And in this case it is perfectly plausible that an outsider (though not necessarily I) would be called in, for who wants to commit an outrage and then have to remain on the scene of the crime? The other reason would be this: you have heard that I ascribe to philosophy "competence in compensating for incompetence"; and if that is supposed to be true in general (you may have reasoned), then it must

87

also hold in the particular case—that is, for the topic of myth; and in that case the author of this semislander of philosophy should show, for once, what he has to offer in this regard.

Very well, then, I have something to offer; and it is a eulogy of polytheism. And in offering this, of course, I am (as it were) carrying owls to Athens—to Athens on the Spree;[a] because the reflections in question are in harmony (and by no means accidentally so) with ideas that Michael Landmann[1] has been in the habit of cultivating, in your competitive marketplace here, much longer than I, and which he has published a number of times: most pointedly, as often with him, in his *Pluralität und Antinomie* [Plurality and antinomy]. What I, for my part, would like to say on this subject now (and in doing so I do not go beyond Landmann, but—probably—too far) I will say in the following four segments: (1) doubts about the striptease; (2) monomythic and polymythic thinking; (3) uneasiness with the monomyth; (4) a defense of enlightened polymythic thinking.

Doubts about the Striptease

Myth is today polymorphously controversial.[b] But here one can safely simplify; or, if one cannot, I shall do it anyway. There are, in my opinion, two basic positions, to begin with, which are at once joined by a third one. The two initial ones have a shared premise. Wilhelm Nestle's successful title, *Vom Mythos zum Logos* [From myth to logos],[2] which was devised as a description of Greek material, seems— going beyond what its author intended—to characterize the course of the world history of consciousness, in its later stage, as a whole. As enlightenment, this history seems to be (and here it does not matter whether this precisely agrees with the sense of Bultmann's formula or not) the great process of "demythologization." In which case myth, whatever else it may be, is at any rate this: something that we are on the point of having put behind us; and the fact that this is the case is either (position 1) good or (position 2) bad. These two positions—the more or less cheerful yes (from Comte to Horkheimer/Adorno and Topitsch) to the demise of myth, and the more or less energetic no (from Vico to the Heidegger school) to it—are more or less inevitably involved, if the world history of consciousness is supposed, at least in its late stage, to be the process of demythologization. But is it really that?

This history of the process of demythologization is, in my opinion, itself a myth; and the fact that, in this way, the death of myth itself becomes a myth, goes some way toward demonstrating myth's relative immortality. It is at least an indication of the fact that we do not get along without myths. This opinion—position 3—is by no means new, either: it is implicit in Lévi-Strauss and also, if I am not mistaken, in Hans Blumenberg, and it has been explicitly advocated by Kolakowski.[3] Without subscribing to the proffered argumentation in every case, I adopt this third position here.

Humankind cannot live without myths; and that should not be surprising, for what are myths? A "mythophile" (which is a description that Aristotle applies to himself) is a person who likes to hear stories: everyday gossip, legends, fables, sagas, epics, travel narratives, fairytales, detective stories, and whatever other kinds of stories there are. Myths, at a very elementary level, are just this: stories. It may be said that a myth is more fictional than a "history" and more real than a "story";[c] but that does not alter the basic fact: myths are stories (*Geschichten*). So anyone who wants to dismiss myth has to dismiss stories, and that cannot be done; because (as Wilhelm Schapp thinks) "we human beings are always entangled in stories"; "the story answers for the person," he writes,[4] meaning every person, and he is right.

It is this—our unavoidable entanglement in stories—that forces us to become the tellers of (these and other) stories; which, given what befalls us, is sometimes the only freedom we are left with: at least to tell, and to color the telling of, that part of the stories that we cannot alter. We also do that when, in the process, we nearly lose track of the story that is in question. Prometheus: here, the person answers for the story that answers for the person. Of course it is a question, why it is that myths sometimes can be so ultrabrief and other times have to unfold what Hans Blumenberg calls "mythical circumstantiality";[5] but either way, it is a question of stories. It is also certainly important to ask whether, as Gehlen thinks,[6] stories become myths when they remain, as it were, "unsaturated," because the empirical identifiability of their personnel is suspended: in which case the actors are place-holders in a "story in itself," whose vacancies are filled, concretely, only when it is received by an audience. In that case, the story stands for everyone; but, clearly, it is still a story. And even if it seems that the core of this story is a "semiological system"[7] and, as it were, disguised mathematics, the issue then is myths, not because these myths are mathematics but because this mathematics is mythical. All of this does indeed introduce differentiations, but at the same time it confirms the basic finding: myths are stories.

Is it not the case, though, that the telling of stories ceases as soon as one has real knowledge? Must myths not disappear where truth appears? But precisely this—it seems to me—is completely mistaken. I do not dispute that myths have in fact entered what was still the empty place in which truth belonged, before humankind had knowledge; but that is an appropriation of something that was intended for other purposes. For myths, when they are not given alien, contramythical functions, are not, in fact, preliminary stages or prostheses of the truth. Rather, the mythical technique—the telling of stories—is some-thing essentially different—namely, the art of bringing available truth within the reach of what we are equipped to handle in life. For the truth is, as a rule, not yet there when it is either (like the results of the exact sciences, as, for example, formulas) too abstract to connect with or (for example, the truth about life, which is death) unlivably awful. In such cases, stories—myths—not only can but must come forward in order to tell these truths into our life-world, or to tell them, in our life-world, at the kind of distance at which we can bear them. For in the last analysis we have nothing that will serve this purpose except sto-ries, especially if what Schelling says is true: "Language itself is only faded mythology!"[8]

The truth is one thing, and how we can live with the truth is another. Knowledge serves the former, cognitively, and stories serve the latter, vitally. For knowledge has to do with truth and error, whereas stories have to do with happiness and unhappiness. Their task is not to find the truth, but to find a modus vivendi with the truth (which—nota bene—is why it is a consolation to know that the poets at least *can* lie).

So when truth comes on the scene, stories—myths—cannot cease, because, on the contrary, it is just then that they have first of all to begin: knowledge is not mythology's grave but its cradle. Because although we do need the "discussed world," we live in the "narrated world."[9] Which is precisely why we cannot live without myths: *narrare necesse est* (to narrate is necessary).

That is, we cannot simply lay myths aside like clothes, although it is also true that laying clothes aside sometimes is not entirely simple. "My identity is my suit," said Gottfried Benn. One of the great Zurich users of textile metaphors—Gottfried Keller—wrote: "Clothes make persons." And if it is nevertheless the case ("the story answers for the person") that stories make persons, evidently clothes that make persons have something to do with stories that make persons; which is why the other great Zurich user of textile metaphors, Max Frisch, wrote in his *Gantenbein:* "I try stories on like clothes."[10] But it does not follow, from Gantenbein's difficulty of choice in view of the riches in his wardrobe of myths, that he is himself only when he no longer has any myth on; and thus it is also not the case that the world history of consciousness is what persons want (as I said in the beginning) to see it as: a striptease called "progress," in which humanity gradually (more or less elegantly) removes its myths and finally (wearing, so to speak, nothing but itself) stands there mythically naked—now nothing but bare humanity. This image is not frivolous, but stays strictly within the framework of the metaphors of the "naked truth," which Blumenberg has investigated.[11] Emil Lask spoke of what was "logically naked"; and similarly one can also speak of what is mythically naked: that is, in the realm of human fundamentals, a naked something that does not exist.

Mythonudism strives for something impossible; because, it seems to me, every demythologization is a well compensated process: the more myths one takes off, the more myths stay on. That is why I have doubts about the striptease: doubts (to put it more precisely) about the idea of the enlightenment (late in world history) as a striptease operating with myths. This idea, I said, is itself a myth; so it is time to find a countermyth to it.

You all know Andersen's socio-psychological fairytale about "The

Emperor's New Clothes," and you remember that clever branch man-
agers in the production and sale of the clothes that make persons had
talked the ruling class into adopting a zero wardrobe. Everything went
well until an impertinent critic of contemporary mores cried out: "But
they don't have anything on!" (That was in the days when criticism
still made a difference.)

In the countermyth that we are looking for now, in our days—
entitled, perhaps, "The Striptease That Was Not a Striptease"—it has
to be the other way around. Here, the mythical zero wardrobe is itself
the explicitly proclaimed goal, and the scientific and emancipatory
avant-garde strives for mythical nudity, and believes that it has
achieved it. And here, it seems to me, everything likewise goes well
only until an impertinent phenomenological hermeneuticist appears
and, *per naivitatem institutam et per doctam ignorantiam* (in educated
naivety and learned ignorance) cries out, "You there, the gentleman
from the late Vienna Circle, you are still wearing myths!" Which is
certainly also very distressing for the person referred to, even if he (if
one thinks, for example, of Ernst Topitsch) is a genuinely talented
storyteller. (How full of myths Topitsch's book, subtitled "The Natural History of Illusion," is, after all;[12] and he also has in common with
the ancient mythologians the way he tells the same story over and over
again.) I grant you: a philosopher who sees through that supposed
striptease, as in fact a masquerade, must indeed be equipped with
sensitive methods. Something as "halfway" as, say, "semi-otics" is by
no means adequate here; one must in fact be "holotically" a hermeneuticist to intervene in this way. But one would, it seems to me, be in
the right: we cannot get rid of stories—of myths; those who think so
deceive themselves. Human beings are subject to myths; a mythically
naked life, without stories, is not possible. To do away with myths is a
hopeless undertaking.

Monomythical and Polymythical Thinking

Contrary to first appearances, these introductory remarks were not
intended to show that enlightenment winds up out of work—that the
task of criticizing myth drops out. For if it is hopeless to try to do away

with myths, it does not follow that there is no longer anything to criticize in myth. Quite the contrary: only now does enlightenment's task of criticizing myth gain precise contours. After all, someone who, in view of the existence of deadly Amanita mushrooms, maintains that we should give up eating altogether, just goes (it seems to me) too far, and will not accomplish anything; a critic of ideology, intent on unmasking, could conclude that such a person has an interest in having other persons starve. Here, after all, the reasonable procedure is the one that was long since, successfully, adopted: to distinguish carefully between what is edible and what is poisonous. The case of myth is just the same: in view of the way in which humans are subject to myths, the critique of myths becomes meaningful and reasonable precisely when one no longer rejects them wholesale, but attempts, instead, to distinguish between wholesome and harmful types of myths, and engages in resistance to the harmful ones.

There are poisonous myths, and I will try to state, here, which they are. My thesis—which is a working hypothesis—is this: what is always dangerous is, at least, the monomyth; polymyths, on the other hand, are harmless. The important thing is that one must be free to have many myths—many stories. Someone who, together with all other human beings, has and can have only one myth—only one story—is in a bad way. So the rule is: *polymythical thinking is wholesome, monomythical thinking is harmful.* Persons who, in their living and storytelling, participate, polymythically, in many stories, are free, by virtue of one story, from the other, and vice versa (and multiply so, in crisscross fashion, by further interferences). Persons, on the other hand, who, monomythically, can and must participate, in their living and their storytelling, in only one myth, do not have this freedom: they are entirely possessed by it—as though by a nonmythical synchronization of mythical entanglements—body and soul. On account of their compulsion to identify completely with this single story, they fall prey to narrative atrophy, and end up in what one can call the unfreedom of identity that results from a lack of nonidentity. On the other hand, the latitude of freedom that goes with nonidentities, which is lacking in the case of the monomyth, is granted by the polymythical plurality of myths. It is a "separation of powers":[13] it separates the power of the story into many stories. By that very means (*divide et impera* [divide and rule] or *divide et fuge* [divide and drive away], at any rate: liberate yourself by separating—that is, by making sure that, as they act on you, the powers that stories are keep each other reciprocally in check, and thus limit this action) humankind acquires the opportunity for freedom that goes with having a manifoldness that is in each case one's own—that is, with being an individual. Persons lose this opportunity as soon as the undivided power of a single story dominates them. In that case—the case of the monomyth—they have to extinguish the nonidentical constitution of their manifold of stories, in the face of this monostory; they submit to the absolute only-myth, in the singular, because this myth commands: I am your only story, you shall have no other stories beside me.

Now in my opinion—for, as a victim of higher education, I know, of course, that in order to talk intelligibly one should provide examples; but here I provide not just an example, but the central, chief, and final example of this phenomenon—in my opinion, then, a monomyth of this sort is the most successful myth of the modern world: the myth of the inexorable progress of world history toward freedom, in the form of the philosophy of history based on the idea of revolutionary emancipation. That—Lévi-Strauss calls it the "myth of the French Revolution"[14]—is a monomyth. Contrary to historicist principles, it suffers no stories beside this one emancipatory world history. Here it becomes apparent that, although one cannot abolish myths, or stories, it is possible, by establishing a monopolistic myth, to centralize and thus depluralize them. That is what occurs here.

In the middle of the eighteenth century—Reinhart Koselleck has shown this by his research in the history of concepts[15]—the philosophy of history (which comes into existence and receives its name then) proclaims "history" in the singular ("*die*" *Geschichte*) as against the previous plural stories or histories (*Geschichten*). Since this "age of singularizations,"[16] in which steps forward (*Fortschritte*) became "progress" ("*der*" *Fortschritt*), freedoms became "freedom," revolutions became "the" revolution, and, as I said, stories or histories became "history"—humankind is no longer permitted to dissipate its energies in individual stories, in which (multi-individually or multiculturally) it takes its various paths toward fuller humanity, but instead from now on it has to hurry purposefully through this single history of progress as the sole possible path to the human goal. We have to pass through this narrow defile, because no other path leads to freedom; this is where we will bring it off, and necessity is on our side; or so it seems, at least. One who withdraws from this single history of emancipation, into individual stories, henceforth becomes a heretic, a betrayer of history, an enemy of humankind. At best, such a one is a reactionary. Thus this monomyth of the history that claims to be no longer "a" history but "history," in the singular, leads to the end of polymythical thinking. I should like to call it the second end of polymythical thinking.

For this second end of polymythical thinking is a late effect of—and the way was long prepared for it by—what one can call, correspondingly, the first end of polymythical thinking. This was the end of polytheism. For polytheism was, so to speak, the classic age of polymythical thinking. The story answers not only for the person, it also answers for the god, which is why in polytheism there were many myths—because there were many gods, who appear in many stories, and of whom many stories could be and had to be told. Polytheism's separation of powers in the absolute—a separation of powers that was accomplished through struggle, and not yet through legal rules—needed, and produced, through polymythical thinking, a separation of powers among stories.

The end of polytheism is monotheism, which is thus the first end of polymythical thinking, and a very specially transcendental (because historical) condition of the possibility of monomythical thinking. In monotheism the one God—precisely by God's uniqueness—negates many gods. In doing so, God at the same time liquidates the many stories of those many gods, in favor of the sole story that is necessary: the salvation story. God demythologizes the world. This occurs, in epoch-making fashion, in the monotheism of the Bible and of Christianity.

It is true that the theologians who are competent here have a habit of pointing, say, to the doctrine of the Trinity and protesting that Christianity—unlike, for example, Islam—is not a "proper" monotheism at all. But it is enough for the context that we are concerned with here that, at any rate, Christianity "acted like" monotheism.

The Christian sole God brings salvation by monopolizing the story. God demands the *sacrificium mythorum* (sacrifice of myths)[17] even before God, within the history of Christian philosophy, finally—at the close of the Middle Ages—gave saving power the image of an anti-worldly dominion of arbitrariness. When, in nominalism, this dominion then demanded, in addition, the world's *sacrifium essentiae* (sacrifice of essence) and humankind's *sacrifium intellectus* (sacrifice of the intellect), this drove humankind and the world into emancipation. When theology expects humankind to remove its head, as well, before God, the head opts for the profane realm; and when the salvation story becomes antiworldly, the world—in sheer self-defense—has to take an antihistorical form. Thus the world is forced—by monotheism itself, indirectly—into storylessness.[18] It takes shape, in the modern age, through the renunciation of even the last story, the salvation story, and thus it takes an antihistorical form, as exact science and as the system of needs; it objectifies itself into a world of mere objects (*Sachen*). Stories, in general, become suspect: myths as superstitions, traditions as prejudices, histories as vehicles of the digressive spirit of mere cultivation (*Bildung*). The end of polytheism—monotheism—demythologizes the world, in effect, into a state of storylessness.

Uneasiness about the Monomyth

But human beings are subject to myths. If that is the case, as I said in the beginning, then this storylessness of the modern world of objectivity (*Sachlichkeitswelt*) is not a gain but a loss, and indeed a loss that cannot be borne. That is why the modern world did not overcome myths and stories, but in fact only created a story deficit: an empty position, a vacancy.

This vacant position is now entered, seemingly irresistibly, by the postmonotheistic monomyth: by the story—proclaimed by the philosophy of history as "history," in the singular—of humankind's revolutionary emancipation (regardless of whether, in utopian fashion, it is treated as a short story, or, in dialectical fashion, it acquires mythical circumstantiality). This new "history"—after God, by way of God's uniqueness, finally withdrew from the world into God's end—is a continuation of the salvation story by partially different means. Like the salvation story—not as its secularization, but as the failure of its secularization—this myth of the termination of myth remains the sole story of the empowerment of a sole power to redeem humankind. But at the same time this monomyth, the "emancipation story," is separated from the Christian salvation story—as its profane copy—by the end of monotheism. So it is historically very late—something found only in modern times—and does not belong to the old mythology, but only to the entirely new one.

The expression "new mythology" came into existence shortly before 1800. "We must have a new mythology," "a mythology of reason," wrote the author of the so-called "Oldest Systematic Program of German Idealism," in 1796.[19] I am one of those who hold to the opinion, first advocated by Rosenzweig and most recently by Tilliette, that this was Schelling.[20] But Schelling, who thus proclaimed the "new mythology," did not (and this strikes me as noteworthy) become the philosopher of the new mythology, but rather of the altogether old mythology. It is true that this is not yet the case in the "system of identity"; there, in the *Philosophy of Art* (Peter Szondi[21] has pointed this out especially energetically), "poets with a calling" and "every truly creative individual" still, for the time being, count as interim agents of the new mythology. Each is supposed "to make for himself a mythology . . . of this [mythological] world that is still in the process of coming into being."[22] But then, after the end of the "system of identity," this call for a new mythology evidently becomes problematic, and finally suspect, for Schelling. It seems that Schelling now discovers, in connection with it, that we do not first have to get the new mythology, because we have already had it for a long time, in unfortunate excess.

For it now becomes apparent, and it continues to become apparent up to our own times, that the new mythology became successful as the mythology of the new: in the myth of progress, of the revolution, of changing the world, of the Reich to come, of the general strike,[23] of the final battle and the final class. In every case, what is in question is a total orientation that is provided by the sole story of the empowerment of the sole power; which is precisely the form of monomyth that becomes possible and dangerous, after Christianity: the absolute sole myth, in the singular, which—as the second end of polymythical thinking—prohibits the plurality of stories, because it now permits only one single story: the monomyth constituted by the revolution story outside which salvation is declared to be impossible. When this new mythology takes hold of the contemporary world, just the aspect of mythology is liquidated that was, after all, freedom: the plurality of stories, the separation of powers in the absolute: the great humane principle of polytheism. Christianity drove it out of the modern world's Sundays, and the new mythology wants to drive it out of our weekdays as well.

Consequently, where the call for a new mythology is answered by a reality and where this begins to be realized, as in the late Schelling, the new mythology brings with it uneasiness about the new mythology. It seems to me that Schelling's late works are already a reaction to this uneasiness: they (literally) distance themselves from the new mythology. That is why Schelling's *Philosophy of Mythology* does not concern itself with the new mythology, but only with the altogether old mythology. And that is why Schelling's *Philosophy of Revelation* attempts to keep the new mythology in its oldest state, so as to possess it as something affirmative;[24] because Christian revelation is, precisely, the oldest new mythology.

Schelling's turning away from the new mythology by turning to the altogether old one is representative of the fate of the interest in myth in the modern world in general. It is marked by uneasiness about the monomyth. When this modern monomyth comes into existence, through the creation of the singular concept of "history," in the period after 1750 that Koselleck christened the "Sattelzeit" ("saddle period," i.e., "transition period"), we immediately see, as a countermove, the formation of an affirmative interest—represented, for example, by Christian Gottlob Heyne—in the polymythical thinking of ancient, and ever more ancient, mythology.[25] When polymythical thinking threatens to follow polytheism in disappearing from our world (a disappearance for which monotheism prepared the way and which the monomyth of the history of progress threatens to put into effect), people seek it—in a mythological turning to the exotic—outside this world: diachronically outside it, in antiquity; or synchronically outside it, in foreign places; best of all, in foreign antiquity. This kind of nostalgic turning to exotic polymythical thinking is carried out by what Carl Otlieb Müller called the *Morgenländerei* ("orientalism") of archeology. Myth research goes back, before classical Greece, to the latter's oriental premises; this is, so to speak, an early and disguised experiment in the mythology of the Third World.

It has, I think, at least three stages. First of all, the investigations of the "dark side" of myth carried out by classical philology, from Heyne and Zoëga through Görres and Creuzer to Bachofen. Then the immanent exoticism of the orientalism surrogate provided by a turning to Germanic mythology, in, for example, Wagner. And finally (after a conversion, so to speak, from Odin to Mao) there is the sinological left-orientalism of our century, which still (in spite of the change from Hafiz to Ho) follows the motto of Goethe's *West-Eastern Divan:* "Flüchte du, im reinen Osten Patriarchenluft zu kosten!" (Make your escape, and in the pure Orient taste the air of the patriarchs).[26]

Today this mythological orientalism takes the forms of Maoism and tourism. Its serious form, which surpasses these, is structural ethnology: the attempt, especially by Lévi-Strauss, to gain distance from the new monomyth of the new by subjecting it to the competition of foreign—polymythical—mythologies, and thus relativizing it.[27] Here one hears everywhere (as Henning Ritter has shown in the case of Lévi-Strauss[28]) the Rousseauvian interest in the noble savage. And it is not enough, then, for that savage to live in antiquity or in the *tristes tropiques* (sad tropics); nostalgia transports him—by means of quotation (for human beings are creatures who quote)—into the most immediate present. When one's break with the establishment was supposed to be demonstrated by one's manner of dress, it was not by accident that persons hit upon the "savage look": the shaggy and bearded persons who were then and are now among us represent, at the apex of modernity, the *bon sauvage* (good savage). The situation is not what the elders, mistakenly, thought; what is passing by, there, are not ungroomed persons but well-groomed quotations from Rousseau.

What is taking place here—the transformation of the most ancient into the most modern; the promotion of the archaic to the avant-garde—can also be observed in other pertinent processes. For example, what Hegel's esthetics—very much in the context of mythological orientalism—identified as art, in preference to the objects that were honored and revered in the argument between the "ancients" and the "moderns" (that is, between "classical" and "romantic" art forms)—the "symbolic art form," as Creuzer's terminology put it, of what Hegel called "abstract" art[29]—becomes, by the beginning of the twentieth century, the watchword of the avant-garde. Within the esthetics of "art forms," it switches, so to speak, from the first to the final period: from the earliest art to the most advanced. Admittedly, even it acquires this avant-garde appeal only by coming to terms with the monomyth of progress and entering its service. This monomyth seems to dominate the contemporary field so much that nothing can live in this field except what adapts and submits to it.

Thus, the overall fate of this countermovement, which is interested in myth, against the new monomyth, is evidently not a happy one. Because the domination of the modern world by the monomyth of the sole story of progress makes its contemporaries uneasy, they seek the lost polymythical thinking in the exotic mythology of prehistory and foreign lands. Because that, evidently, is not sufficient, an attempt is made to transform it into something present. In the process, however, this old mythology ceases to be that for the sake of which one sought it. It loses its polymythical character by submitting to the monomyth of the new, and thus it finally only confirms the latter's power. Thus the countermeasure, here, is outlived by what induced it: by uneasiness about the monomyth. From which, it seems to me, we can conclude that the interest in exotic mythology, both ancient and foreign, is a symptom, but not a solution.

A Defense of
Enlightened Polymythic Thinking

Consequently, if we are to arrive at a solution, alternative countermeasures have to be considered. That, too, I want to do here only in the form of a brief sketch. Here I am not abandoning the topic of myth, I am only extending the radius of attention to matters relating to myth; because attending only to exotic, ancient, and foreign mythology involves the danger of obstructing attention that could be paid to pertinent modern phenomena. That then leads to an artificially partial characterization of the present, in which nothing is seen but what I have addressed so far: the modern "objectification," which is storylessness, and its (then seemingly irresistible) compensation by the new monomyth. But the present includes more, and mythologically, at any rate, it does not include only monomythical thinking; because (and this is my concluding thesis, here, in regard to myths) *there is also a kind of polymythical thinking that belongs specifically to the modern world.*

This modern kind of polymythical thinking is what we have to bet on, in order to turn our uneasiness with the monomyth in a productive direction. For it is not only the case that the monotheistic demythologization is the indirect empowerment of the new monomyth; it is in fact also the case that in modern times, specifically, the monotheistic demythologization launches what it meant to liquidate: polymythical thinking. How does that come about? Perhaps in this way: monotheism disenchanted and negated polytheism, and polymythical thinking along with it. But the modern world begins—as I suggested earlier—with God's withdrawing from the world, into God's end: that is, it begins with the end of monotheism. As with other phenomena that monotheism apparently vanquished (for example, fate), this end of monotheism creates a new opportunity for polytheism and for polymythical thinking. One might say that while it leaves them still disenchanted, it negates their negation. In other words, precisely in the modern world polytheism and polymythical thinking—being disenchanted—are able to return: as enlightened polytheism and as enlightened polymythical thinking. I would like to point to three findings that belong in this context.

First, there is *the disenchanted return of polytheism.* Polytheism's modern—profane, intraworldly—aggregate state is the political separation of powers. The political separation of powers is enlightened—secularized—polytheism. It does not first begin with Montesquieu, with Locke, or with Aristotle; it already begins in polytheism: as the separation of powers in the absolute, through the pluralism of gods. It was monotheism that forbade them heaven and thus also contested their rights on earth. But because the God who, for Christianity, was one, and who negated the many gods, withdrew from the world at the beginning of the modern age, into God's end, God did not only liquidate heaven. At the same time, by doing this, God made the earth, the this-worldly world, free for a return (of course, now, a disenchanted, no longer "divine" return) of the many gods. When biblical monotheism expelled them from heaven, it only banished them, in effect, to the earth, where they established themselves as the gods—no longer divine now, but institutions—of the legislature, the executive, and the judiciary; as the institutionalized struggle of organizations in the process of political will-formation; as federalism; as the competition of economic powers in the market; and as the endless differences of theories, of worldviews, and of decisive values. "The many old gods ascend from their graves; they are disenchanted and hence take the form of impersonal forces. They strive to gain power over our lives and again they resume their eternal struggle with one another."[30]

Secondly, there is *the genesis of the individual:* the individual draws life from this separation of powers.[31] The individual comes into existence in opposition to monotheism. As long as, in polytheism, many gods were powerful, individuals (if not threatened by a monopolistic political power) had latitude by virtue of the fact that they could always be excused, in relation to one god, by the service they owed another one, and thus they could be (moderately) inaccessible. A certain amount of untidiness, produced by the collision of the ruling powers, is necessary in order for humans to have this free space; a minimum amount of chaos is a condition of the possibility of individuality. But as soon as, in monotheism, only a single God rules, with a single salvation plan, humankind has to enter God's total service and totally obey. This is a situation in which humans have to constitute themselves explicitly as unique individuals and provide themselves with inwardness, in order to make a stand. They thwart omnipotence by means of ineffability. That is why polytheism did not discover the individual: it did not need it, because there was as yet no monotheism there to present an extreme threat. But monotheism, for its part, did not itself discover the individual, but only (though of course this was

not a minor accomplishment) provoked that discovery, because it—
monotheism—really endangered the individual for the first time. That
is why it was only after monotheism that the individual could come
forward publicly, and why it was only in modern times, with the
secularized polytheism of the separation of powers, that one could
really have the freedom to be an individual. One risks this freedom
when one submits, monomythically, to a new monopolistic power.
Then, fascinated by the new myth of the sole history, one sticks to the
path that is only supposedly the path to heaven on earth, and is in
reality the path to the identity, on earth, of heaven and hell: to an
integrated, all-purpose eternity.

The individual needs, in the third place, the *disenchanted return of polymythical thinking*, in order to make a new stand here. One
needs it in order to fulfil one's inescapable obligation to myth, but to
fulfil it not monomorphically and progressively, by means of an absolute sole story, but rather polymorphically and transgressively, by
means of many relative stories. There is, as I said, a type of polymythical thinking that belongs specifically to the modern world. This, in
particular, has to be emphasized: the common rejection of a definition
of myths as stories—a rejection that one finds equally in Roland
Barthes and in Alfred Baeumler[32]—is only a device by which to restrict
myths to the realm of the exotic and to exclude the possibility that the
present produces its myths as well. The more myths are understood,
on the contrary, as stories, the more one can see that there is a specifically modern polymythical thinking. Here I will mention only two of
the forms that it takes: the scientific study of history, and the esthetic
genus, the novel.

These are specifically modern phenomena,[33] and they investigate or
invent—at any rate, they tell—many stories. Monotheism obliterates
the many gods from the stories, and its end obliterates the one God
from them, as an acting, central figure, as well. Thus in modern times
the—disenchanted—myths make (in every respect) the step into prose:
from the cult into the library. There the history books and novels are
present as the polymyths of the modern world. That, too, is enlightened polytheism. They are "enlightened" in that, for one thing, fiction
and reality seek different genera, even if in the historians' stories of

reality there are (when they remain historians and write history in a narrative manner) inevitable remnants of fiction, and in the novelists' fictions there are (even, and especially, after the modern disenchantment of the epic into the "epos of the God-forsaken world"[34]) *fundamenta in re* (bases in reality). Histories and novels are the—enlightened—polymyths of the modern world.[35] One has to seek dealings with them in order to find one's way back, from the "useful idiocy" into which the ignorance-guiding anticognitive interest[e] of monomythically inspired direct utopian action seduces one, to the cautious prudence of education (*Bildung*): the education that grants equality of opportunity to stories—to (*non-engagé*) history and to (*non-engagé*) literature, the liquidation of which produces the vacuum into which the monomyth forces its way. It is time, in view of the bad continuation of monotheism by monomythical thinking, to stand up for the modern stories in the plural—the historiographical and the esthetic stories—and, in this sense, for an enlightened polytheism, which protects individual freedoms by separating even the powers that stories are.

If you will allow me one final observation: all of this might not be without consequences for philosophy as well. It seems to me that it is also time for philosophy to end its collaboration with the monomyth and to gain distance, as well, from everything in itself that disposes it in favor of such collaboration. By this I mean in particular the conception of philosophy as an orthological mono-logos: as the singularizing attempt to empower a sole reason by means of prohibitions of dissent, an attempt in which stories, as incorrigible mischief-makers, are a priori not admitted, because in them persons narrate rather than coming to agreement. It seems to me that it would be good to regain, toward that kind of orthology, the loose relationship that Mark Twain recommended when he said that he pitied anyone who did not have the imagination to spell a word now one way and now another. A philosophy is a sad science if it is not able to think now one thing about a subject and now another, and to let this person think (and go on thinking) one thing and that person something else. In this sense, even the "single idea" that occurs to one (*der Einfall*) is suspect. Long live the multiple idea (*der Vielfall*)!

Stories have to be permitted again. What is well thought is already halfway to being a story, and maybe someone who wants to think even better should go the whole way. Philosophy has to be permitted to tell stories again, and of course to pay the price for that: the price of acknowledging and putting up with its own contingency. But here one already anticipates the cries of horror and the indignant warnings from the guild: that this means relativism—with the well-known paradoxes and fallacies that go with it—and is bound to end badly, or even end in skepticism. There was once a skeptic who heard these warnings and did not perceive them as objections. What do they mean, anyway, he murmured, when he realized that this warning was addressed to him (but for reasons of prudence he only murmured it)? What do they mean, why am I a skeptic? I like fallacy.ᶠ Here I stand, and I can always do otherwise. I tell stories (as a kind of Scheherezade, who, it is true, now has to tell them against his own mortality)—I tell stories, so I still am; and that is (exactly) why I tell them: stories, and speculative short stories, and different histories of philosophy, and philosophy as stories, and more stories, and (where myth is concerned) stories about stories; and if I have not died, I am still alive to this day.

Notes

1. M. Landmann, "Polytheismus," in his *Pluralität und Antinomie* (Munich/ Basel, 1963), pp. 104–50; cf. idem, *Pluralistische Endzeit* (Stuttgart, 1971), pp. 147ff.

2. W. Nestle, *Vom Mythos zum Logos. Die Selbstentfaltung des griechischen Denkens von Homer bis auf die Sophistik und Sokrates* (Stuttgart, 1940).

3. C. Lévi-Strauss, *Das wilde Denken* (1962) (Frankfurt a.M., 1973), esp. pp. 302ff. (in English, *The Savage Mind* [London, 1966]). On the basic pattern of Lévi-Strauss's argument—that what modern persons do not want to be, they stylize as the other, the distant "nature" and the "savage," but they do not thereby cease to be it—see idem, *Rasse und Geschichte* (1952) (Frankfurt a.M., 1972), esp. pp. 16ff. (in English: *Race and History* [Paris, 1952]). An exemplary application of this analysis is his *Totemism* (1962) (Boston, 1963), and see the whole of his *Mythologiques* (pp. 1964ff.), esp. vol. 4, *The Naked Man* (New York, 1981), esp. pp. 652ff.: myth cannot die without being resurrected immediately in music. Hans Blumenberg's text is "Wirklichkeitsbegriff und Wirkungspotential des Mythos," in M. Fuhrmann, ed., *Terror und Spiel. Probleme der Mythenrezeption* (Poetik und Hermeneutik, 4) (Munich, 1971),

pp. 11–66, and see pp. 527ff. See also Blumenberg, *Work on Myth* (1979)(Cambridge, Mass., 1985). L. Kolakowski's text is *Die Gegenwärtigkeit des Mythos* (second printing, Munich, 1974).

4. W. Schapp, *In Geschichten verstrickt. Zum Sein von Mensch und Ding* (Hamburg, 1953), pp. 1 and 103. For the way this approach is currently being appropriated, see H.Lübbe, *Geschichtsbegriff und Geschichtsinteresse. Analytik und Pragmatik der Historie* (Basel/Stuttgart, 1977), esp. pp. 145ff., 168ff., in which emphasis is placed simultaneously on the (primary and dominant) way in which stories are things that "happen to us" (esp. pp. 54ff.), and on the way in which they constitute a "culture of the experience of contingency" (pp. 269ff.).

5. Blumenberg, "Wirklichkeitsbegriff," pp. 43ff.

6. A. Gehlen, *Urmensch und Spätkultur. Philosophische Ergebnisse und Aussagen* (Frankfurt a.M./Bonn, 1964), esp. p. 222.

7. R. Barthes, *Mythologies* (1957) (London, 1972), p. 111.

8. F. W. J. Schelling, "Philosophie der Mythologie" (lectures delivered from 1820 onward), in *Sämtliche Werke*, ed. K. F. A. Schelling, part 2, vol. 2 (Stuttgart/ Augsburg, 1857), p. 52. So the role of myth here is not only to retell alien things so as to make them familiar, but equally to put terrifying things at a distance. I have tried to formulate a characterization of myth as a procedure for creating distance and for sparing oneself in my synopsis of H. Blumenberg's theses, in Fuhrmann, *Terror und Spiel*, pp. 527–30.

9. H. Weinrich, *Tempus. Besprochene und erzählte Welt* (1964)(second printing, Stuttgart/Berlin/Cologne/Mainz, 1971).

10. M. Frisch, *Mein Name sei Gantenbein* (1964) (Hamburg, 1968), p. 19.

11. H. Blumenberg, *Paradigmen zu einer Metaphorologie* (Bonn, 1960) (reprinted from *Archiv für Begriffsgeschichte*, 6 [1960] 7–142), pp. 47–58.

12. E. Topitsch, *Mythos—Philosophie—Politik. Zur Naturgeschichte der Illusion* (Freiburg, 1969).

13. See H. Schelsky, *Systemüberwindung—Demokratie—Gewaltenteilung* (Munich, 1973), esp. pp. 55ff.

14. Lévi-Strauss, *The Savage Mind*, p. 254; cf. idem, *Anthropologie structurale*, vol. 1 (Paris, 1958), p. 231: "Nothing resembles mythical thought more than political ideology does. It is possible that in our contemporary societies the latter has simply replaced the former." (A somewhat different translation: *Structural Anthropology* [New York, 1963], p. 205.)

15. Summed up now in R. Koselleck, "Geschichte, Historie," in O. Brunner, W. Conze, and R. Koselleck, eds., *Geschichtliche Grundbegriffe. Historisches Lexikon zur politisch-sozialen Sprache in Deutschland*, vol. 2 (Stuttgart, 1975), esp. pp. 658ff.

16. R. Koselleck, "Historia magistra vitae. Über die Auflösung des Topos im Horizont neuzeitlich bewegter Geschichte," in H. Braun, and M. Riedel, eds.,

Natur und Geschichte, Karl Löwith zum 70. Geburtstag (Stuttgart/Berlin/
Cologne/Mainz, 1967), p. 265. Translated in Koselleck's *Futures Past.
On the Semantics of Historical Time* (Cambridge, Mass., 1985).

17. This very simplified account undoubtedly pushes the monomyth and the Christian salvation story too close together. My acknowledgment that Christianity is not a "proper" monotheism, but only "acted like" monotheism, is meant to allude to the fact that the Christian salvation story remained, or became, a comparatively liberal "sole story," which did tolerate—and even inspired—collateral stories (and, to that extent, polymythical thinking). But it seems to me that polymythical thinking remains unofficially present even in the most radical and most intolerant monomythical thinking. The revenge of polymythical thinking that is monomythically suppressed is the joke.

18. On the concept of the "storylessness" of modern society, see J. Ritter, "Hegel und die französische Revolution" (1957), in his *Metaphysik und Politik* (Frankfurt a.M., 1969), esp. p. 227 (translated in Ritter, *Hegel and the French Revolution* [Cambridge, Mass., 1982]); idem, "Subjektivität und industrielle Gesellschaft" (1961), in his *Subjektivität* (Frankfurt a.M., 1974), esp. p. 27, and idem, "Die Aufgabe der Geisteswissenschaften in der modernen Gesellschaft" (1963), in the same volume, esp. pp. 130ff.

19. In R. Bubner, ed., *Das älteste Systemprogramm. Studien zur Frühgeschichte des deutschen Idealismus* (Hegel-Studien, Beiheft 9) (Bonn, 1973), p. 265.

20. F. Rosenzweig, *Das älteste Systemprogramm des deutschen Idealismus. Ein handschriftlicher Fund.* 1917 (Sitzungsberichte der Heidelberger Akademie der Wissenschaften, Stiftung Heinrich Lanz, Phil.-hist. Klasse, Abhandlung 5) (Heidelberg, 1917). X. Tilliette, "Schelling als Verfasser des Systemprogramms?" in Bubner, *Das älteste Systemprogramm*, pp. 35–52.

21. P. Szondi, "Antike und Moderne in der Ästhetik der Goethezeit" (1961–1970), in his *Poetik und Geschichtsphilosophie*, vol. 1 (Frankfurt a.M., 1974), esp. pp. 238–39, and 225ff. See also Szondi in Fuhrmann, ed. *Terror und Spiel*, pp. 639–40.

22. F. W. J. Schelling, "Philosophie der Kunst" (1802–1805), in *Sämmtliche Werke*, part 1, vol. 5 (1860), pp. 444–46.

23. G. Sorel, *Über die Gewalt* (1906) (Frankfurt a.M., 1969), esp. pp. 141ff. In English: *On Violence* (Glencoe, Ill., 1950).

24. F. W. J. Schelling, "Philosophie der Mythologie" (from 1820 on), "Philosophie der Offenbarung" (from 1827 on). I hope that the interpretation I have suggested here is compatible with W. Schulz's *Die Vollendung des deutschen Idealismus in der Spätphilosophie Schellings* (Stuttgart, 1955), esp. pp. 304–6.

25. On what follows, see K. Gründer, introduction to J. Bernays, *Grundzüge der verlorenen Abhandlung des Aristoteles über Wirkung der Tragödie* (Hildesheim/New York, 1970), pp. viff.; E. Howald, ed., *Der Kampf um Creuzers*

Symbolik. Eine Auswahl von Dokumenten (Tübingen, 1926), pp. 1–28 (editor's introduction); A. Baeumler, "Bachofen, der Mythologe der Romantik," in M. Schroeter, ed., *Der Mythos von Orient und Occident. Eine Metaphysik der alten Welt aus den Werken von J. J. Bachofen* (2nd ed., Munich, 1956), pp. xxii–ccxiv; and K. Kerenyi, ed., *Die Eröffnung des Zugangs zum Mythos. Ein Lesebuch* (Darmstadt, 1967).

26. Goethe, "Hegire," lines 3–4, from *West-östlicher Divan* (1819); translated by David Luke in *Goethe* (Baltimore, 1964), p. 230.

27. C. Lévi-Strauss, *Tristes Tropiques* (Paris, 1950), pp. 423–24 (trans. as *A World on the Wane* [London, 1961], p. 391): "knowing [other societies] better does none the less help us to detach ourselves from our own society. It is not that our society is absolutely evil, or that others are not evil also; but merely that ours is the only society from which we *have* to disentangle ourselves."

28. H. Ritter, "Claude Lévi-Strauss als Leser Rousseaus," in W. Lepenies and H. Ritter, eds., *Orte des wilden Denkens* (Frankfurt a.M., 1970), pp. 113–59.

29. G. W. F. Hegel, "Vorlesungen über die Ästhetik" (1818 on), in *Werke in 20 Banden* (Theorie-Werkausgabe), E. Moldenhauer and K. M. Michel, eds., vol. 13 (Frankfurt a.M., 1970), pp. 107ff., 389ff.

30. M. Weber, "Science as a Vocation," in H. Gerth and C. W. Mills, eds., *From Max Weber: Essays in Sociology* (New York, 1958), p. 149 (trans. slightly revised). Compare Landmann, *Pluralität und Antinomie*, pp. 129–32.

31. Compare Schelsky, *Systemüberwindung*, p. 57: "What this principle of the separation of powers produces for the situation and behavior of individual human beings . . . is a . . . protection of the individual in relation to all power-constellations. . . . The individual's vital interests, in their multiplicity, contradictoriness, and individualization, are protected above all by virtue of the fact that for the most diverse regions of his life, he finds political advocates and patrons who act on behalf of his interests, in each case, in a businesslike manner, with commitment, and without regard to whether he is part of the majority or the minority of voters in regard to the political regime at the time—that is, without regard to which party he belongs to or whom he voted for. To put it concretely: my freedom as an individual consists in the fact that with my vote in parliamentary or regional elections I have not also decided who will represent my interests as an employee or an official, as a parent or a listener to the radio, as a house-owner or a saver, and that in all of these regions of my life I encounter decision-making and administrative agencies that are preprogramed to disregard my politics. The multiplicity of institutions in a society that make decisions on their own "political" authority—the institutional pluralization of power—provides the decisive guarantee for the individual's freedom to be able to pursue his various interests and claims on life in a way that is relatively "free of domination" (*Herrschaftsfrei*)."

32. Barthes, *Mythologies*, p. 151: "Myth deprives the object of which it speaks of

all history. In it, history evaporates." By this, Barthes wants to justify his
statement that "Statistically, myth is on the right" (p. 148)—which I doubt,
and which in turn Barthes can only support by means of a supplementary
error: "left-wing myth is inessential" (p. 147). For Baeumler, see his "Bachofen" essay, p. xci: "Myth is utterly unhistorical."

33. This is shown, for the sense of history, by Ritter, "Die Aufgabe der Geisteswissenschaften in der modernen Gesellschaft," in his *Subjektivität*, esp. pp. 120ff.,
and by Lübbe, *Gechichtsbegriff und Geschichtsinteresse*, esp. pp. 304ff. H.
Blumenberg elucidates the novel's "belonging . . . to the [modern age's] concept of reality as immanent consistency" in his "Wirklichkeitsbegriff und
Möglichkeit des Romans," in H. R. Jauss, ed., *Nachahmung und Illusion*
(Munich, 1964), pp. 9–27.

34. G. Lukács, *Die Theorie des Romans* (1920) (Neuwied/Berlin, 1971), p. 77.
(*The Theory of the Novel* [Cambridge, Mass., 1971]). On the correlation
between myth and historiography, compare Lévi-Strauss, *The Raw and the
Cooked* (New York, 1969), p. 13: "history, as its clear-sighted practitioners
are obliged to admit, can never completely divest itself of myth." On the
correlation between myth and the novel, compare his *The Origin of Table
Manners* (New York, 1978), esp. pp. 130–31.

35. C. Lévi-Strauss puts music in a center position here (see *The Naked Man* [New
York, 1981], pp. 652ff.), and writes (expanding what he wrote in the "Over-
ture" to *The Raw and the Cooked*, esp. pp. 15ff.): in "the modern age, when
the forms of mythic thought were losing ground in the face of the new scientific knowledge, and were giving way to fresh modes of literary expression . . .
music took over the structures of mythic thought at a time when the literary
narrative, in changing from the myth to the novel, was ridding itself of these
structures. It was necessary, then, for myth as such to die for its form to escape
from it, like the soul leaving the body, and to seek a means of reincarnation in
music. In short, it is as if music and literature had shared the heritage of myth
between them. Music, in becoming modern with Frescobaldi and then Bach,
took over its form, whereas the novel, which came into being about the same
time, appropriated the deformalized residue of myth and, being henceforth
released from the constraints of symmetry, found the means to develop as a
free narrative. We thus arrive at a better understanding of the complementary
natures of music and the novel, from the seventeenth or eighteenth centuries to
the present day." In general: "With the death of myth, music becomes mythical
in the same way as works of art, with the death of religion, are no longer
merely beautiful but become sacred" (p. 653); it was with Wagner that this
situation first became a conscious one (pp. 653–54); and thus "at least during
this period of Western culture," "music, in its own way, has a function compa-
rable to that of mythology," as "a myth coded in sounds instead of words"
(p. 659).

Translator's Notes

a. The Spree is the river with which Berlin is associated—where the colloquium at which this paper was presented took place.

b. *Polymorph kontrovers*—an untranslatable pun on Freud's concept of the "polymorphous perverse."

c. "History" and "story" are both in English in the original, because this contrast is not so readily available in German (where *Geschichte* does duty for both of them).

d. *Unbehagen am Monomythos.* The distinctive term *Unbehagen* (which I translate as "uneasiness") happens to be the same one used by Freud in the title of the book we know as *Civilization and its Discontents* (*Das Unbehagen in der Kultur*).

e. *Ignorierensleitende Ignoranzinteresse*, a satirical variant of Jürgen Habermas's *erkenntnisleitende Wissensinteresse*.

f. This sentence is in English in the original.

6

The Question, To What Question Is Hermeneutics the Answer?

Hermeneutics is the art of getting out of a text what is not in it. Otherwise—since after all we have the text—what would we need it for? But do we need it at all? What exactly is it that we need when we need interpretation, when we need hermeneutics? How must, how can, hermeneutics itself be understood and interpreted?

I am one who comes, as a skeptic, from the hermeneutic school and has never quite escaped it, but instead, remaining within it—as (so to speak) an endogenous Trojan Horse—is more and more strongly inclined to think that the core of hermeneutics is skepticism and the important form of skepticism today is hermeneutics. One with such a background must sooner or later confront the question what hermeneutics is. This then becomes, to a certain extent, the search for an answer to my question of what I am, with the attendant temptation not to find one. Of course this private motive is hardly a respectable reason to request that people pay heed to my subject. It is nonetheless permissible to do this because there are also other reasons for returning again to this much-discussed topic, hermeneutics. I would like to elucidate some of these reasons in what follows, and I would like to do so in seven sections. To begin with, I will name them: (1) question and answer; (2) finitude; (3) hermeneutics as a reply to derivativeness; (4) hermeneutics as a reply to transitoriness; (5) literary hermeneutics as a

reply to the civil war over the absolute text; (6) its apparent obsolescence; (7) hermeneuticists and code-breakers. At the head of my discussion I place the motto: "Read and let read!"[a] and I begin it—entirely
conventionally—with the first section.

Question and Answer

The question, formulated at the outset, as to what hermeneutics is, is
itself a problem of understanding, itself a hermeneutic question.

Hans-Georg Gadamer, appealing to Collingwood, emphasized the
importance of the reply structure for the hermeneutic business of interpretation:[1] one understands something by understanding it as an answer to a question. To put it differently, one does not understand it if one
is not aware of and does not understand the question to which it was or
is the answer. Since then Hans Blumenberg[2] has drawn our attention to
more complicated possibilities associated with this schema of question
and answer. For example, it can be the case that the question correspond-
ing to a solution has died out, historically, so that the solution adopts
substitute questions, as an answer to which it can again become intelligible. Blumenberg confirms the question/answer schema by differentiat-
ing it. I consider this reply-model of understanding—with the additional reason that at the ninth colloquium on poetics and hermeneutics,
last year, Hans Robert Jauss again energetically put forward the
question/answer schema as the basic hermeneutic schema of the theory
of (literary) reception[3]—to be generally important and correct. I am not
disturbed in this by the suspicion, which has in the meantime been
expressed occasionally, that the definition of this historical linkage relationship as a quasi-linguistic relationship of reply is questionable, because it is merely a metaphorical manner of speaking. I certainly admit
that committed attempts at "demetaphorization" remain unsatisfying:
Ricoeur's action-as-text theory,[4] for example—the revenge of hermeneutics on the text-as-action theory[5] of the "speech-act" camp—rather
strengthens the suspicion of metaphor. Nevertheless, the objection I
have mentioned does not alarm me. I simply accept the conclusion that
the question/answer schema is a metaphor. For if it is a metaphor, it is
undoubtedly a good one, a fruitful one. And every philosophy is bound

to employ metaphor. Just as with grog, where one can have water, should have sugar, and must have rum, so with philosophy, one can have formalization, should have terminology, and must have metaphor. Otherwise it is not worth it—in the first case, worth drinking, and in the second, worth philosophizing.

From all this and much else it follows—it seems to me—that if the question of what hermeneutics is (which today always also has to be the question why literary hermeneutics is the dominant form of hermeneutics) is a hermeneutic question and must be answered hermeneutically, then the question/answer schema, which stems from Collingwood and Gadamer—which seems to be the worked-out form of the linkage that Joachim Ritter entitled "hypoleptic"[6]—is central for this. This question/answer schema is then not only the schema *with which hermeneutics operates in order to understand things*. It is also at the same time—for that very reason—the schema *with the help of which hermeneutics itself can and must be understood*. Consequently one who intends a hermeneutic clarification of hermeneutics has to ask, in turn: What were and are the questions to which hermeneutics itself— and to which the contemporary dominance of literary hermeneutics— was and is the answer? To put it another way: the *hermeneutic* question of what hermeneutics is is *the question: To what question is hermeneutics the answer?*

Finitude

My fundamental thesis on this subject is not surprising, for a hermeneutic philosophy, but more nearly trivial. It is that *hermeneutics is a reply to human finitude*. In connection with this thesis—which, however trivial, is still in need of elucidation—human finitude must be connected to *time*, if it is to do justice to the following characteristics of hermeneutics: plainly, one understands and interprets only things that *are already there*—even one who interprets anticipations interprets actual anticipations, not future ones—so that *hermeneutics is primarily a relationship to the past*.[7] So when a philosophy lays stress on hermeneutics, the temporal condition must obtain that the past, and the past in particular—at least as a past that puts an imprint on the present: as *derivation (Herkunft)*—is essential.

Here one should not allow oneself to be abashed by the fact that this does not suit those philosophies for which only the *future* is essential, to such an extent that they only value, in the past, what "has not been requited":[8] that which, in the wishes of what is past, was what even today is still only future. The philosophies of history—from the revolutionary ones to those which are only still hoping—are philosophies of the future. For them human beings, directly or indirectly, pursue an emancipation leading to a state of wholeness, the completion of history. For that, to be sure—to put it quite simply—humans (at least their avant-garde) would need omniscience, infinite goodness, and omnipotence. They lack these, however, because they are finite. Precisely this leads to the great experiences of disappointment for the philosophy of history: to the disappointment of emancipatory "immediate expectation"[b] by which the contemporary situation of philosophy is also, and indeed especially, determined. For that reason philosophy nowadays is again attentive to human finitude; and it is so by once again making hermeneutics fundamental. The philosophers of history have only *changed* the world, in various ways—the point is, to *spare* it[c]—but the form of sparing that changes the most is interpreting.

So hermeneutics urges finitude. In the process, it makes a fact into a question,[9] by being the answer to it: specifically, to human finitude. But what does this mean: finitude? I will now sketch briefly *three* mutually compatible *concepts of finitude,* so as to bring out their outlines by contrast, before I go on to make use of the third one.

Finitude can be defined:

1. *In relation to God.* This is done theologically: What is finite is what is not God, what is nothing by itself, and therefore only exists through God—that is, the created. In philosophy this is the metaphysical tradition's concept of finitude: *to be finite is to be something created.* Finitude can also (more or less nontheologically) be defined:

2. *In relation to space.* This is done above all in modern philosophical anthropology, and there representatively by Helmuth Plessner: in his *Die Stufen des Organischen und der Mensch* [The levels of organic life and man] he defines the finite as the bounded (with a different

relationship, in each case, to its boundary).[10] This definition of finitude by a boundary lives on today in the fundamental role assigned by systems theory to the differentiation between a system and its surrounding world.[11] It is fruitful for analyses of the reaction of the bounded thing to threats to its boundary that it meets with. As "boundary reactions"[12] of this kind we can understand, in living things, the immune system (Thomas A. Sebeok), in human beings, anxiety (Thure von Uexküll), laughing and crying (Plessner), history's "cultivation of the experience of contingency" (Hermann Lübbe), literary texts as ways of digesting a "boundary infringement" that is called an "event" (Jurij M. Lotmann), and so forth.[13] But all of these "boundary reactions" derive their existence from the fact that there are boundaries, that is, that there is finitude; and finitude here—understood from the perspective of space—means the elementary nonubiquity of what is bounded: *finitude is being one thing among others.* Finitude can also (more or less nontheologically) be defined:

3. *In relation to time.* This is done above all in the modern philosophy of existence, and there representatively by Heidegger, specifically in *Being and Time:*[14] something is finite if its time is meted out, runs out, ends—through death. That is the definition of finitude by means of a temporal ending, which is the basis of the principle that *finitude is mortality,* and human finitude is conscious mortality: *Being toward death.*

Only this third concept of finitude explicitly brings finitude together—as I required of a concept of finitude that would be important for hermeneutics—with time. Therefore, in what follows I will operate with it, and with it in particular, in explicating my fundamental thesis—that hermeneutics is a reply to human finitude—and thus perhaps make that thesis a little more exciting. In doing so I must, of course, at the same time resolve the seeming paradox that the importance (in relation to hermeneutics) of the past is supposed to be guaranteed by a concept of finitude that brings into play precisely a future—everyone's future—namely, death. In any case it follows that *hermeneutics,* if it is a reply to finitude, *is a reply to death.* But death exists for us in two forms: as *one's own death,* and as *the death of others.*[15] Depending on which death hermeneutics replies to, it is either a reply to *derivativeness (Herkömmlichkeit,* which I will discuss in the third section) or a reply to *transitoriness* (which I will discuss in the fourth section).

Hermeneutics as a Reply to Derivativeness

The paradox I just mentioned is not really a paradox, because the situation with the past and with the future that is *one's own death* is as follows: *because* we die and we know this, we are referred to our past. Everyone's future is "authentically"[d] their death: life is short, *vita brevis*. This shortage of time for the human being—the *moriturus* (being going to die) that knows itself as *moriturus*—delivers it over to what it already was, to its derivation. Very simply: on account of the shortness of human life, no human being has the time in which to distance itself from the past that it is, to whatever extent it would like. Everyone always remains predominantly his or her own derivation, which while it is, historically, contingent—that is, could also have been different—is not (for the one who is it) contingent in the sense of an arbitrariness that can be chosen and rejected at will, but rather in the sense of a fate that can be escaped only with difficulty or hardly at all. The "choice that I am"[16] includes, unavoidably, the past that is the history of my derivation, as the nonchoice that I am. This unavoidability of always remaining predominantly what they already were, which is imposed on human beings by their mortality, I entitle "derivativeness."

Humans resist this derivativeness: they want to *change*. The motive that propels them in this can be designated in various ways: as the thirst for freedom, as curiosity, as a longing for the happiness that lies in surrender to what is entirely "other" and to that extent new, as "fear of missing something,"[17] as the desperation of derivation that results from a deficiency of future, as temporal claustrophobia, and so on. But—*vita brevis*—humans do not succeed in changing everything; they try in vain to get free of their derivation: even the revolutionaries—following the apt formulation of Olof Palme—are, on the day after the revolution, at best reformists: they have to link up with what is there. For the derivativeness that is determined by finitude, which is to say by mortality, is the foundation of the antiprinciple of "linking up." In every future that is produced by a process of change there remains a quantity, always greatly exceeding the quantity of change, of derivation. This antiprincipled principle^e of historical inertia implies, I think, not only the expediency of incrementalism but also, for the very same reason, the inevitableness of Martin Kriele's well-known rule of the burden of proof.¹⁸ Nonchange is always so very much the greater part that, on account of the shortness of our life, it exceeds our capacity for rational justification. If, then, under the conditions of deadline-pressure that are imposed by our *vita brevis*, one wants to justify anything rationally at all, one must obey Kriele's rule and justify not nonchange but change: the burden of proof is on the one who makes changes. So derivativeness dominates change: predominantly, humans just do not get free of their historical derivation. What they can change is always less than they want to change and is never everything, but always precisely not the greater part.

Hermeneutics is an answer to this situation of finitude determined by mortality, *an answer to this derivativeness;* for hermeneutics is a way of changing where no change is possible. Here one must *do something else*—namely, *interpret*. In doing this—*vita brevis*—the interpretive attempt to get free that is embodied in "unmasking" interpretation (that is, in the critique of ideology) is only possible within limits. Any global unmasking is done at the cost of a regression of the unmasker. The critique that throws suspicion on everything easily makes the critic naive on a second level, serving, so to speak, as the continuation of stupidity by means of intelligence. But this unmasking interpretation is, anyhow, only the extreme limiting case of what interpretation—as a reply to derivativeness—normally accomplishes, which is to remove the historical derivation that (as a world of texts or as a paratextual world of tradition) confines us and sustains us, to a distance at which we can get along with it. Thus hermeneutics is the art of putting things into a bearable relation to oneself. This sort of interpretation, which makes up for the impossibility of doing away with derivation by providing the possibility of distancing oneself from one's derivation, I call *distancing hermeneutics*. It is a reply to *derivativeness*, and it is more prevalent the more the desire to change things, and the limiting experiences pertaining to that desire, are prevalent. In other words, it is quite modern.

Here again, the rule holds true: we do not succeed—our life is too short—in distancing everything by means of interpretation. There are things that cannot be distanced, things that (for example, as what is 'usual')[19] people simply repeat in the process of living—in other words, things that we do not interpret, but just are. Derivativeness, then, is in the last analysis indissoluble. As the question to which hermeneutics is the answer, derivativeness is always bigger, as a question, than hermeneutics can be as an answer.

Hermeneutics as a Reply to Transitoriness

I repeat: because we die, we always remain predominantly our past. We *cannot* get free of our derivation to whatever extent we would like—but we *should not* get free of it to whatever extent we would like, either. No one—life is too short for this—can reorder, from the ground up, what affects them in this life. That is always too much for a being whose capacity for overcoming things is limited because it always dies all too soon. For that reason, derivativeness is not only a burden for humans but also—and perhaps still more—a shelter.[20] So an arbitrarily large amount of change cannot be expected of humans. Future requires derivation. In every future that is produced by change, a minimum of derivation, far exceeding the quantity of change, must be preserved. Otherwise the change miscarries, and the ones for whose sake one wanted the change—humans—are destroyed. For this antiprinciple of linking up, however, the second form of death—*the death of others*—creates difficulties, seeing that *with every death, some of the intelligibility of past things, for those who remain alive, dies.* Anyone who has ever had to care for the estate or for the literary remains even (in fact especially) of close relatives—the primeval situation (I think) of the historian—knows what I mean. Our derivation, without which we cannot live, continually slides—through the death of others—into unintelligibility: its intelligibility escapes us. Here I entitle this "transitoriness."

Humans resist this transitoriness. They have to *hold fast*, to *preserve*. The motive that propels them in this can be designated in various ways: as the need for continuity and the obligation of identity, as a longing for the happiness that lies in self-preservation, as "fear of losing something,"[21] as the desperation of the future that results from a deficiency of derivation, as temporal agoraphobia, and so forth. But—*vita brevis*—humans do not succeed in preserving everything. They try in vain to retain the immediate intelligibility of what they derive from, seeing that no one lives long enough to transmit to those who survive them everything that they themselves understand. That holds also and especially where—in the modern world—the expected lifespan increases in length. For precisely here, on account of the modern increase in the rate at which skills in understanding also become obsolete,[22] the expected life span of any individual's effectiveness in transmission declines rapidly at the same time. So the modern world radicalizes transitoriness. Thus, through the death of others and through the obsolescence of their skills in conveying orientation (an obsolescence that accelerates in modern times), the historical derivation that humans after all are escapes faster and faster into unintelligibility.

Hermeneutics is an answer to this situation of finitude determined by mortality, *an answer to this transitoriness*. For hermeneutics is a way of holding fast where one cannot hold fast. Here one must *do something else*—namely, *interpret*. In doing this, the attempt to hold fast by means of antiquarianizing interpretation—by collecting—is a gesture that is just as symptomatic as it is helpless, seeing that in this matter it is not sufficient to seek antiquities and perhaps find hundreds in Germany "and, in Spain, one thousand and three."[23] But this antiquarianizing interpretation is, anyway, only the extreme limiting case of what interpretation, as a reply to transitoriness, normally accomplishes: namely, to save the intelligibility of things and of texts in new situations (in secondary contexts), to which it adapts them.[24] It has, then, a conserving effect: a rehabilitation of old buildings, so to speak, in the realm of the spirit. This sort of interpretation, which makes up for the loss of primary intelligibility by rendering things intelligible again, I call *adapting hermeneutics*. It is *a reply to transitoriness*, and it is more prevalent the more the alteration of reality accelerates and thus produces more and more loss-of-familiarity, that is to say, strangeness. This is the case in the modern world. Because in this world, in particular, in which our derivation and our future—in other words, our life-world and our science-world (the world of tradition and the world in which we meet our needs)—become separated to an exceptional degree, there arise precisely in it (as compensation, as Joachim Ritter says) the hermeneutic or cultural sciences (*Geisteswissenschaften*).[25] The more rapidly everything in today's reality continually changes, the more the art of becoming familiar with something again—hermeneutics—becomes a necessity, generated by this speed.

In the process, through the modern increase in the tempo of change, it also receives exceptional opportunities. It seems to be the rule that the increase in the speed at which things become obsolete is compensated for by an increase in the prospects for old things being reactivated.[26] Consequently, for example, part of the modern world is the cycle of waves of nostalgia: in the realm of theory, for example, from systems theory via Neo-Marxism to the recent boom in evolutionary theory, with the necessity of adapting these, hermeneutically, to the continually changing state of the world. Thereby, at the same time, the opportunity for gaining something new through hermeneutics arises: because in today's world everything that is most our own, being subject to the tempo of change, almost immediately becomes foreign, and by the same token what is foreign—and consequently even the most exotic world of the past—winds up at the same, normal remove from us as what is most our own, and in that way becomes equally accessible for the hermeneutics that became necessary, in the European world, for the reactualization of what was most our own. The result is that today, through interpretation, we can recollect even what we never forgot, because we did not even know it yet; and thus, hermeneutically, we regain the paradise from which we were never driven out, because we had never been born into it. We gain, through hermeneutics, a second-level openness to the world.[27] So the modern world is not only the age of radicalized transitoriness, but also at the same time the age of the radicalized answer to the question that transitoriness is: it is also the true age of adapting hermeneutics.

Literary Hermeneutics as a Reply to the Civil War over the Absolute Text

But what is the question to which, not hermeneutics (distancing and adapting) in general and taken as a whole, but specifically the modern *literarization* of hermeneutics is the answer? I have bypassed this problem up to this point, even though I have by no means already treated hermeneutics—by reference to death, that is, to finitude as derivativeness and as transitoriness—only as an anthropological magnitude and, as it were, an unvarying answer, but have also very definitely treated it—by reference to its specifically modern fortunes—as a historical magnitude and as an answer to which a date can be attached. So that very state of affairs has remained unclarified, which, however, virtually cries out for clarification: I refer to the fact that hermeneutics, precisely, in the course of its modern fortunes, becomes, absolutely centrally, *literary hermeneutics*. It becomes the art precisely of the *literary* reader's understanding of the *literary* text. At present only literary hermeneutics counts as "hermeneutics" in the general sense, whereas theological and juristic hermeneutics function as mere auxiliary arts in disciplines having only specialized competence.[28] How does this come to be the case?

In considering this problem it is, I think, useful to keep in mind from the beginning that (if we leave aside Aristotle's *Peri hermeneias*, which is another matter) the term "hermeneutics" first becomes the title-concept of a book—that of Dannhauer[29]—in 1654: that is, not only well after the Reformation's proclamation of the rule of scripture and not only shortly after the appearance of Descartes' fundamental writings,[30] but also immediately after the end of the Thirty Years' War. Thus I advance a conjecture that—although this may only demonstrate my ignorance in this regard—I have not yet found in the literature, although it is a natural one: *the question (or at least one question) to which the literarization of hermeneutics was the answer is the experience of religious civil war.*

Of course hermeneutics, as a phenomenon to which a date can be attached and as a developed art, does not first occur then and in modern times, but already occurs earlier—namely, at least (at the very latest) when Christianity established itself as a church and in the process needed and (appropriating the devices of Homeric exegesis and the tricks of application of Roman law) developed a technique by which to establish the one correct reading, and, so to speak, the one absolute reading (for salvation) of the *Bible*. This theological

hermeneutics had always to rediscover—figuratively or allegorically
or by dogmatic abstraction—in the many biblical stories the one
necessary story, the story of redemption, and thus always—and for
this purpose the assumption of at least a double sense of the text was
indispensable—in the manifold "letter" of scripture the single "spirit."[31] I would like to entitle this "singularizing hermeneutics" and to
distinguish it from "pluralizing hermeneutics,"[32] which—in reverse—
traces out many possible meanings and the most various kinds of
spirit in one and the same literal form. Singularizing hermeneutics,
then, calls the multiformity of the literal stories to the order of the
one sole absolute meaning and spirit: it belongs, as the self-assertion
of orthodoxy against heterodoxy and heresy, to the difficult phase of
the institutional establishment of the religion.

Now it is important, I think, to see that theological hermeneutics
initially remained a singularizing hermeneutics even when, as a result
of the Reformation, the rule of tradition and the rule of scripture came
into conflict with one another: the dispute there was between two
singularizing hermeneutics, for both wanted the correct interpretation,
with its significance for salvation, of the absolute text, the holy scrip-
tures. I will resist the temptation, which would be natural from my
considerations up to this point, to treat this dispute between Catholic
and Protestant hermeneutics as an extreme case of the opposition
between adapting and distancing hermeneutics. Instead I will emphasize immediately that the moment in which the scale was tipped between singularizing and pluralizing hermeneutics first arrived when
this hermeneutic dispute became *bloody,* and in fact for generations: in
the religious civil war, which was, at least among other things, a
hermeneutic war—a *civil war over the absolute text.* Here death again
became significant for hermeneutics: this time the violent finitude,
death as killing, "being toward killing" (*"das Sein zum Totschlagen"*),
to use this formula of Koselleck's[33] in a way that is relevant here. My
thesis is that *hermeneutics gives an answer to this experience of the
deadlines of the hermeneutic civil war over the absolute text by
inventing—thus turning itself into pluralizing, which is to say literary,
hermeneutics—the nonabsolute text and the nonabsolute reader:* in
other words the text and the reader that (except in the case of those

anticipators, the humanists) had really not existed before—namely, the *literary text* and the *literary reader*.

The dogmatic quality of the claim to truth that is made by the unambiguous interpretation of the absolute text can be deadly: that is the experience of the religious civil wars. When, in relation to the sacred text, two interpreters assert, in controversy, "I am right; my understanding of the text is the truth, and in fact—and this is necessary for salvation—in this way and not otherwise": then there can be hacking and stabbing. Hermeneutics, when it turns into pluralizing hermeneutics, gives an answer to precisely this situation when it asks: Could this text not be understood, after all, in still another way, and—if that is not sufficient—still another way, and again and again in other ways? In this way it takes the edge off potentially deadly controversies about interpretation, by transforming the dogmatic relationship to the text into the interpretive one: into an understanding of the text that is open—*ad libitum*, if necessary—to discussion: and someone who is open to discussion may possibly stop killing. The hermeneutics that transforms itself in this way into a pluralizing hermeneutics *does something else:* it replaces "Being toward killing" with Being toward the text—that is, with Being toward a conciliatory text, and the value of this kind of hermeneutics lies in the fact that it allows us to avoid and spare ourselves this textual homicide. This means making the text, also, tolerant in matters of the "will to power" through historical influence. This conciliatory understanding of the text, in its most consistent—that is, its most conciliatory—form, is the literary reader's Being toward the literary text. The latter arises, then—through the literarizing of hermeneutics—as a reply to the deadly conflict over the absolute understanding of holy scripture. Part of this genesis of the neutral reader—in what was also an age of *hermeneutic* neutralizations[34]—is the search for the context that relativizes the controversy over the absolute understanding of the text in favor of what is uncontroversial, or controversial without consequences, in the understanding of the text.

In this connection the history of the origin of literary hermeneutics is traversed by two fundamentally different positions. Spinoza, in the *Tractatus*, makes *knowledge of nature* the final authority in the interpretation of scripture: from which it follows—at the latest, when knowledge of nature becomes exact natural science—that hermeneutics is presumed to be superfluous.[35] The approach initiated by Romanticism turns against this: Schleiermacher—understanding the Bible as literature among other literature[36]—discovers as the fundamental situation of pluralizing or literary hermeneutics the conversational sociability of the *endless discussion,* which allows everyone to have their say, without any time limit and without any compulsion to reach agreement: differently, then, than in the so-called dominance-free discourse, which of course makes everyone a servant of the pressure for consensus—that is, in practice, a servant of whoever administers the pressure for consensus.[37] *Originalitas, non veritas, facit interpretationem* (originality, not truth, makes something an interpretation.)[f]

For the rest, because hermeneutics becomes literary hermeneutics, because it is pressed by the fear of violent death, its key concept becomes nondeath, or *life:* the talking and letting-talk of the endless discussion (which includes reading and letting-read) serves living and letting-live. It seems to me just as attractive as it is called for, now, to reconstruct the concept of life in the hermeneutics associated with Dilthey's "philosophy of life"[38] in terms of this formulation, and also to find the tendency that is defined by this formulation in Gadamer's approach that takes play as its point of departure,[39] an approach that defines human existence as Being toward the text, toward the literary text, which (as Jauss's version of the theory of recognition has urged) can always be read in yet another way and can also always have yet another meaning, because it has no "meaning in itself," but rather—through delight in the context—is capable of endless interpretation.[40] So this—literary—text now becomes the paradigm of hermeneutics; *literary hermeneutics*—by transforming the absolute text into the literary text, and the absolute reader into the esthetic reader—*is given precedence,* as a reply to the hermeneutic civil war over the absolute text.

Its Apparent Obsolescence

I consider the predominance of literary hermeneutics to be something we cannot relinquish: but that opinion—by Zeus!—nowadays is not in step with the times.

For at present a *discomfort with the precedence of literary hermeneutics*[41] prevails everywhere, and in fact (I think) *because*—for the modern world's increasing speed of change increases its forgetfulness—*the question is forgotten to which this rise of literary hermeneutics was the answer:* the danger of hermeneutic civil war. Consequently—that is, because the Thirty Years' War seems very far away and the French Revolution at least far enough away that the Terror begins to be a problem that one can skip over—consequently literary hermeneutics and its primacy today seem obsolete, as perhaps a relic of the notion of the "educated middle classes." Once, following the sly thesis of, among others, Lutz Geldsetzer,[42] the Reformation became academically successful through the hankering of the theological faculty to become the philological one. Today the reverse hankering is at work. The philologists would like to be theologians, with all the trimmings: holy writings, ecclesiastical office of instruction, orthodoxy and heresy, index, banning, excommunication, and also, as far as possible, with a devil, whether the devil is now called capitalism or something else. The study of literature wants to return from the literary and disengaged position back to the position of involvement, from pluralizing hermeneutics back to absolute, singularizing, hermeneutics.

Of course today one can no longer employ the existing theologies of Christianity for this tendency to return to theology, for they have both— and I emphasize: both (being philologically educated and enlightened with regard to literature)—long since passed through the Reformation and have both long since assimilated the reply to its consequences of conflict as well: both of them. A theology that today is still pre-Reformation in character must be sought elsewhere. And one finds it, in the modern *philosophy of history,* which, strictly speaking, is not a secularized theology,[43] but rather the only theology in regard to which secularization, so far, has failed. In it, singularized hermeneutics rules, the reason being that the philosophy of history, following Koselleck's familiar thesis,[44] arose as a result of singularization: because in all the many stories it allowed validity to only one single story, "history,"[g] the concept of which it invented somewhere around 1750, and which it defined as the intraworldly history of redemption through emancipation. This philosophy of history needs singularizing hermeneutics in order—repressing the polymythical multiplicity of the many stories and demanding the monomythical simplicity of the one history—once again to discover and to promote, in all "dealings" and actions and thoughts and texts, the one absolute history. In this way—that is, by depluralizing and deliterarizing hermeneutics—it makes hermeneutics a matter of creed again and thus—this is the point—again makes it able and eager to get into a situation that it seemed to have behind it: into hermeneutic civil war.[45]

The *revolutionary* philosophy of history, then, does not act toward the danger of that civil war in a manner that seeks to avoid it; on the contrary, one must—that is (frequently unconsciously) its answer—*not avoid* the civil war, *but win* it, as a revolution. Of course, in order to be able to win it, one must have it; and when one has it, one must go through with it, in bloody and deadly fashion, perhaps again for entire generations: and is it worth this? Does it produce anything at all desirable? There one has, I think, to consider at least three things: the doubtfulness of actual victory; that which comes before the victory; and that which comes after the victory. The prognosis on all three points is, in my opinion, always bleak. For the rest, one should not—as those persons do, most innocently, who present themselves as world champions of suspicion—one should not depend upon one's own harmlessness, unless this (precisely in the removal of the consequences of thought from one's sphere of concern) is institutionalized with sufficient security.

I think, then, that in view of the perennial danger of neoreligious hermeneutic civil war, it is not the singularizing hermeneutics of the philosophy of history but the pluralizing procedure of literary hermeneutics—which I dare say covers historiography as well—that is called for and, as I said, is not something that we can relinquish. It is the answer that lives and lets live by reading and letting read. Taken by itself it is certainly not sufficient in this regard, but it is necessary—which was all that was at issue here. This literary hermeneutics, as a pluralizing hermeneutics, operates with liberalism's technique of the *separation of powers,* in accordance with which the individual—while no doubt he cannot, using Adorno's formula, "be different *without* fear"—can at any rate be different with *reduced* fear, ultimately—*divide et fuge!*[h]—by separating the powers of texts and interpretations as well—that is, by dividing even the authorities that stories[46] are, and separating even the powers that texts are.

Hermeneuticists and Code-Breakers

One who wants to clarify hermeneutics *hermeneutically* must pose the question of the question, or of the questions, to which hermeneutics is the answer; and such a person must attempt to answer it, in the way that I have attempted (partially) to answer it here, or in a different way, or still another way, or yet again another way. In this use of the question/answer schema—nota bene—the question in each case (and thus also the question to which hermeneutics is the answer) is the condition of the possibility of the answer and of its intelligibility, so that the hermeneutic question of what this question is is something to which the transcendental philosophers actually think they have the exclusive right—namely, a question about "the conditions of the possibility" of something. In hermeneutics, these conditions are *historicized;* hermeneutics *makes the transcendental point of view into the historical one.*[47] Of course, there is still the question whether in reality one *must* proceed hermeneutically in order to understand, and to conceptualize, what understanding and interpreting are.

That is at least not self-evident. There is at present again an alternative to the hermeneutic approach, one that in conclusion I would like to take up briefly here—in particular because hermeneutics, it turns out, is also the answer to it. This alternative is *code-breaking.* It has been on the advance—also and especially as a theory of understanding—under various scientific names (as communication theory, as semiotics, and so forth) for some time. The question of understanding is then—as perceived by the "sender" and by the "receiver"—that of the code that is being used. Today the analysis of the conceptual history of the basic unit of vocabulary in the human sciences that are no longer diachronic is, in general, a hermeneutic desideratum: Why, for example, in this approach does the decisive concept of possibility ("competence") come from the realm of words associated with rivalry,[48] and the decisive concept of actualization ("performance") from the realm of images

associated with the theater? In regard to the "code" concept I suspect—
a suspicion that is subject to refutation—that although "code" (as co-
dex: for example in the *Code Napoléon*) had long since changed from a
word designating manuscripts and books to one referring to a list or a
summing up of rules, it probably only became a prominent fundamental
term (by way of linguistics) beginning with the moment at which, following the invention of the radio (Marconi, 1897), the decoding of the
enemy's encoded radio messages (and the encoding of one's own) became, to a significant extent, the task of military experts in secret languages: *"code" begins its career in linguistics as a word associated with
espionage.* From this time onward—on a grand scale since, at the latest,
the First World War—the expert in decoding and encoding can become
the key member of the group of linguistic scientists (a group who in
times of war are not uncommonly engaged in this kind of activity) and
"code" can increasingly become the key term of linguistics and then also
of the study of literature and of society. But that means that *with the
increasing popularity of the code concept the perspective of the decoder
becomes the characteristic perspective of the human sciences:* the perspective of one who is confronted with language as "secret language,"
as the language that I do *not* speak, do *not* understand (in contrast to the
mother tongue and to the languages that are usually acquired in school,
languages that, in general, I *already* speak and understand). Under the
pressure, too, of the increasing demands made by ethnology—and of
the special problem of decoding dead systems of hieroglyphic writing—
the relationship to the language that is *not* understood, to the text that is
not understood, to the *fait social* ("social fact") that is *not* understood,
becomes exemplary for linguistics and for the studies of literature and
society. Adorno[49] strikingly contrasted Max Weber's sociology based
upon "understanding" (*verstehende Soziologie*) with Emile Durkheim's
sociology of *faits sociaux,* and interpreted the Durkheimian sociology
as the sociology of a world that has become unintelligible: it is significant that the father of modern linguistics, Saussure, took his orientation
from Durkheim.

However: as a rule, while it is never the case that we understand
everything, neither is it the case that we understand nothing at all.
We only understand what we already understand.[50] Therefore, in my

opinion, the code-breaking theory of understanding (in other words, the nonhermeneutic theory) betakes itself methodically and artificially out of the (phenomenologically privileged) situation in which we exist in our daily life-world—that is to say, out of the situation of the *always* or (as the case may be) *in each case already* (somehow) understood or preunderstood language, world of texts, or social world. But this language or world is precisely what hermeneutics takes as its point of departure. The code-breakers start from a fundamentally foreign, nonunderstood world, whereas the hermeneuticists start from a fundamentally familiar, already understood world: *therefore the authority to which hermeneutics appeals is not a "code," but history.* There are advantages to this. It is easier to hold fast to diachronic problems, which the code-breakers have mostly not left behind but only banished into problem-exile. Thus, for example, today the history of words is studied, in the form of the history of concepts, by nonlinguistic hermeneuticists—that is, by philosophers and historians.[51] I do not know whether the linguists, who formerly were responsible for this subject and who in ten years at most will yearn to have the assignment back, will get it back then (unless they wisely never gave it up at all).

Hermeneutics, then, is an answer to code-breaking, in that, in compensatory fashion, it preserves the problems that code-breaking represses—including the problem of the *hermeneutic* clarification of hermeneutics. Thus its advantage lies not only in the fact that it links up with the phenomenologically privileged life-world situation, in which we always find ourselves already understanding things, but also in the fact that, because it can appeal to the wealth of understanding contained in pregiven understandings (to the "preinterpretedness" of the world), it preserves problems. Hermeneutics is able to do this because it is closer to the concrete, the interesting, the gripping—the dateable—questions. To put it in terms of the image of mountain climbing, while hermeneutics always already has its base-camp of preunderstandings close beneath the ridge crest of concrete problems of understanding—thanks to history, which brought the camp to that point—code-breaking sciences must constantly begin at the bottoms of the valleys at the foot of the problem-mountain, at zero or even at a negative level. While the code-breaking science does then (placing high demands on means of financing) unflinchingly traverse the stretches on which one needs much apparatus, many Sherpas and many scientific assistants, the question is still whether it actually and often reaches the problem-slopes on which the hermeneuticists are always almost immediately—mostly without the oxygen-mask of research subsidy—on their way, in small roped parties or alone.

I conclude my discussion with the following: the poor hermeneuticists—I hear others besides code-breakers say—never get out of history. But *must* one then get beyond history? One who does not get out of history, does not arrive at an absolute position. But *must* one then arrive at an absolute position? One who wants to be a philosopher without an absolute position commits unspeakable fallacies. "I like fallacy."[i] But one who says that will come to a bad end or even end—laden with contradictions—as a skeptic. This well-intentioned warning is unlucky: the skeptic that I am not supposed to become, I already am; and for that very reason—because skepticism is not successful when one advocates no thesis at all, but rather (as a separation even of the powers that convictions are) when, at any given time, one advocates too many theses—for that very reason I have advocated here the theses that I have advocated, which also include the opinion expressed at the beginning, that the core of hermeneutics is skepticism and the important form of skepticism today is hermeneutics.

Notes

1. H.-G. Gadamer, *Wahrheit und Methode. Grundzüge einer philosophischen Hermeneutik* (Tübingen: Mohr/Siebeck, 1st ed. 1960, 3rd ed. 1972), pp. 344ff., esp. 351ff., or *Truth and Method* (New York, 1975), pp. 325ff., esp. 333ff. See R. G. Collingwood, *An Autobiography* (Oxford, 1939; 3rd ed. 1978), pp. 29ff.
2. Hans Blumenberg, *Die Legitimität der Neuzeit* (Frankfurt, 1966).
3. H. R. Jauss, "Überlegungen zur Abgrenzung und Aufgabenstellung einer literarischen Hermeneutik," in H. R. Jauss, ed., *Text und Applikation* (Munich, 1981). My essay explicates ideas from my introduction to the discussion of this contribution in Bad-Homburg on May 27, 1978. See my statement under the same title in the cited volume.
4. P. Ricoeur, "Der Text als Modell: hermeneutisches Verstehen" (1972), in H.-

G. Gadamer/G. Boehm, eds., *Seminar: Die Hermeneutik und die Wissenschaften* (Frankfurt, 1978), pp. 83–117.

5. K. Stierle, *Text als Handlung* (Munich, 1975).

6. J. Ritter, *Metaphysik und Politik. Studien zu Aristoteles und Hegel* (Frankfurt, 1969), pp. 64ff.; compare G. Bien's article, "Hypolepsis," in J. Ritter, ed., *Historisches Wörterbuch der Philosophie* (Basel/Stuttgart), vol. 3 (1974), cols. 1252–54.

7. This is in conscious contrast to M. Heidegger, *Sein und Zeit* (Halle, 1927), pp. 336ff., or *Being and Time* (New York, 1962), pp. 385ff. and his thesis that "understanding is grounded primarily in the future" (*Sein und Zeit,* p. 340, compare p. 339; *Being and Time,* 390, compare 388–89).

8. Compare E. Bloch, *Das Prinzip Hoffnung,* vol. 1 (Berlin, 1953), p. 19: "because [this philosophy] knows no past whatsoever except the past that is still alive, that has not yet been requited," it is a "philosophy of the future, that is, also of the future in the past."

9. In this form I appropriate the critique that H. Krings (in H. M. Baumgartner, ed., *Prinzip Freiheit* [Freiburg/Munich, 1979], esp. pp. 391ff.) directed at my plea against a "concept of freedom that is restricted to one, futuristic half" (p. 337; compare 322ff.). The difference that is decisive in this regard does in fact fall short of pure unconditionality and sheer givenness.

10. H. Plessner, *Die Stufen des Organischen und der Mensch. Einleitung in die philosophische Anthropologie* (Berlin/New York [1st ed., 1928, 3rd ed.], 1975), esp. pp. 99ff., 123ff.

11. Compare esp. N. Luhmann, "Funktionale Methode und Systemtheorie" (1964), in his *Soziologische Aufklärung. Aufsätze zur Theorie sozialer Systeme* (Opladen, 1974), pp. 31–53, esp. 38ff. (see above all the statements regarding the "system-boundary," p. 40).

12. H. Plessner, "Lachen und Weinen. Eine Untersuchung der Grenzen menschlichen Verhaltens" (1941), in his *Philosophische Anthropologie* (Frankfurt, 1970), esp. pp. 155ff.

13. T. A. Sebeok, "The Semiotic Self," and T. von Uexküll, "Positionspapier," both so far unpublished discussion pieces for the roundtable discussion "Semiotik der Angst" (Bad Homburg, Dec. 8–11, 1977); H. Plessner, "Lachen und Weinen," cited in note 12; H. Lübbe, *Geschichtsbegriff und Geschichtsinteresse. Analytik und Pragmatik der Historie* (Basel/Stuttgart, 1977), esp. pp. 20, 54ff., and 269ff.; J. M. Lotmann, *Die Struktur literarischer Texte* (Munich, 1972), p. 332—compare the following pages and pp. 311ff.

14. M. Heidegger, *Sein und Zeit,* esp. pp. 235ff., 245ff., 329ff.; or *Being and Time,* pp. 278ff., 289ff., 377ff.

15. M. Heidegger, *Sein und Zeit,* pp. 237ff.; or *Being and Time,* pp. 280ff.; and W. Schulz, "Zum Problem des Todes," in A. Schwan, ed., *Denken im Schatten des Nihilismus* (Darmstadt, 1975), pp. 313–33, esp. 331ff.

16. "Le choix que je suis": Jean Paul Sartre, *L'être et le néant* (Paris, 1943), p. 638.

17. Compare P. Probst, *Politik und Anthropologie. Untersuchungen zur Theorie und Genese der philosophischen Anthropologie in Deutschland* (Frankfurt, 1974), pp. 40ff. With this reference and the one in note 21 I would like to indicate what I can't enlarge on here: that the duality of "derivativeness" and "transitoriness" is connected to the duality of types of fear that is analyzed by Probst and to the duality of versions of happiness (self-surrender and self-preservation) that is analyzed by R. Spaemann, "Philosophie als Lehre vom glücklichen Leben," in G. Bien, ed., *Die Frage nach dem Glück* (Stuttgart, 1978), esp. pp. 15ff.

18. M. Kriele, *Theorie der Rechtsgewinnung* (Berlin, 1967), summing up on 312: "presumptive binding force of prior judgments. There is a (refutable) presumption in favor of the rationality of all prior judgments." See the same author's *Die Herausforderung des Verfassungsstaats* (Neuwied/Berlin, 1970), esp. pp. 18–20; also N. Luhmann, "Status quo als Argument", in H. Baier, ed., *Studenten in Opposition. Beiträge zur Soziologie der Hochschule* (Bielefeld, 1968), pp. 73–82, esp. 78: "involuntary conservatism deriving from complexity"; also H. Lübbe (vol. cited in n. 13, above), pp. 329ff.: "Tradition is valid not because of its demonstrated correctness but because of the impossibility of getting along without it," so "that in relation to tradition, there must be an initial presumption of its rationality, and the burden of explicit argument lies on the person who rejects it."

19. Compare my "Über die Unvermeidlichkeit von Üblichkeiten," in W. Oelmüller, ed., *Normen und Geschichte* (Paderborn, 1979), pp. 332–42.

20. Compare the concept of "supportedness" (*Getragenheit*) developed, in opposition to Heidegger's "thrownness" (*Geworfenheit*) by O. Becker, "Von der Hinfälligkeit des Schönen und der Abenteuerlichkeit des Künstlers," in the Husserl festschrift *Ergänzungsband* to the *Jahrbuch für Philosophie und phänomenologische Forschung* (Halle, 1929), pp. 27ff.

21. P. Probst (vol. cited in n. 17), 40ff. (compare n. 17).

22. As a result of the increasingly rapid obsolescence of experiences; this results, among other things, in the emergence, as characteristic traits of the modern world, of the victory of "anticipation" over "experience"—see R. Koselleck, *Vergangene Zukunft. Zur Semantik geschichtlicher Zeiten* (Frankfurt, 1979), or *Futures Past. On the Semantics of Historical Time* (Cambridge, Mass., 1985)—and the phenomenon of the forfeiture of experience: H. Lübbe, "Erfahrungsverluste und Kompensationen. Zum philosophischen Problem der Erfahrung in der gegenwärtigen Welt," *Giessener Universitätsblätter* 2 (1979) pp. 42–53.

23. There are not only erotic Don-Juanism and Don-Juanism in the choice of psychiatrists but also a Don-Juanism of antiquarianizing: it is a contributing motive in the genesis of the museum. On the theory of the museum and of its

genesis, precisely in the modern world, see J. Ritter, *Subjectivität* (Frankfurt, 1974), esp. pp. 126ff.

24. Compare K. Gründer, "Hermeneutik und Wissenschaftstheorie," *Philosophisches Jahrbuch* 75 (1967/68), p. 155: "Between the utterance that is to be understood and the person who would like to understand it there lies a historical break, by virtue of which the person who would like to understand has stepped out of, has emancipated himself from, the historical context to which the utterance belongs. Hermeneutics is the theory of understanding under the difficulties imposed by emancipations."

25. J. Ritter, "Die Aufgabe der Geisteswissenschaften in der modernen Gesellschaft," in the vol. cited in n. 23; compare H. Lübbe, *Geschichtsbegriff und Geschichtsinteresse* (cited in n. 13), esp. pp. 304ff.

26. See my "Kompensation. Überlegungen zu einer Verlaufsfigur geschichtlicher Prozesse," in K. G. Farber and C. Meier, eds., *Historische Prozess* (Munich, 1978), esp. pp. 349ff.

27. See my "Felix culpa? Bemerkungen zu einem Applikationsschicksal von Genesis 3," in H. R. Jauss, ed., *Text und Applikation* (cited in n. 3), sec. 5.

28. On the diagnosis of this situation, see H.-G. Gadamer, *Wahrheit und Methode*, esp. pp. 307ff., or *Truth and Method*, pp. 289ff.

29. J. C. Dannhauer, *Hermeneutica sacra sive methodus exponendarum sacrarum litterarum* (Strassburg, 1654). It is not my thesis that this is a literary hermeneutics: rather, it belongs in the tradition of the theological hermeneutics of, for example, M. Flacius, *Clavis Scripturea Sacrae* (1657), which faces up to the burdens resulting from the Reformation's rule of scripture (*sola scriptura*). Compare also H. E. H. Jaeger, "Studien zur Frühgeschichte der Hermeneutik," *Archiv für Begriffsgeschichte* 13 (1974), pp. 35–84.

30. R. Descartes, *Discours de la Méthode* (1637); *Meditationes de prima philosophia* (1641). H.-G. Gadamer writes in his article, "Hermeneutik," in J. Ritter, ed., *Historisches Wörterbuch der Philosophie* (Basel/Stuttgart), vol. 3 (1974), col. 1062: "When we speak of hermeneutics today, we stand ... in the scientific tradition of the modern age. The use of the term 'hermeneutics' that corresponds to that tradition begins precisely at that time, that is, together with the genesis of the modern concept of method and of science." While I do not dispute this, I still think that the turning that leads to method is only a partial motive for the modern trend toward hermeneutics, because it is only one version of "neutralization" among others.

31. See 2 Corinthians 3:6; commentary in G. Ebeling, "Geist und Buchstabe," *Die Religion in Geschichte und Gegenwart* (3rd ed., Tübingen, 1958), cols. 1290–96. On the history of the substitution of multiple kinds of interpretation for the multiple meaning of scripture, see H. R. Jauss (article cited in note 3); on figurative interpretation compare, in the history of literature, E. Auerbach, *Mimesis. Dargestellte Wirklichkeit in der abendländischen Literatur* (Bern/

Munich [1st ed., 1946, 6th ed.], 1977), esp. pp. 75ff., and in philosophy K. Gründer, *Figur und Geschichte. J. G. Hamanns "Biblische Betrachtungen" als Ansatz einer Geschichtsphilosophie* (Freiburg/Munich, 1958), esp. pp. 93ff.

32. See my "Schwacher Trost," in H. R. Jauss, ed., *Text und Applikation* (cited in n. 3).

33. R. Koselleck, "Kriegerdenkmale als Identitätsstiftungen der Überlebenden," in O. Marquard and K. Stierle, eds., *Identität* (Munich, 1979), p. 257.

34. On the concept of the "Age of Neutralizations," see C. Schmitt, *Der Begriff des Politischen* (1922, 1934; Berlin, 1963), 79ff., or *The Concept of the Political* (New Brunswick, N.J., 1976). These neutralizations include not only the genesis of the state that is neutral with regard to creed, and the rendering autonomous of "morality," "economics," and "technology" as neutralizing powers, but also the development of a hermeneutics that is neutral with regard to theology: the detheologizing of juristic hermeneutics (putting it also under the motto of the principle of Albericus Gentilis cited by C. Schmitt, *Der Nomos der Erde* (Cologne/Berlin, 1950), p. 96: "Silete theologi in munere alieno"), the desacralization of the Bible, which turns it into a piece of literature, and in general the genesis of the neutral—that is, the literary—reader. Perhaps this neutralization, as the modern fate of hermeneutics, is possible only under the protection of the modern neutralization of the state, and—I am using points of view developed in a conversation on this subject with B. Willms—the formation of the literary "author" only under the protection of the neutral state's *auctoritas*.

35. In my opinion, B. Spinoza's *Tractatus theologico-politicus* (1670) carries out the "turning toward the historical," which H.-G. Gadamer ascribes to him (in his article, "Hermeneutik," cited in n. 30), only in an instrumental way; for it mainly serves to turn potentially deadly points of contention in the interpretation of scripture into matters of indifference (that is, to defuse them) within the framework of a program of demythologization that makes rational "knowledge of nature" the standard for the understanding of the Bible. The result—where nature is "disenchanted" out of the pantheistic equation with God into the object world that can be experimented with and mathematized, and knowledge of nature becomes the exact knowledge of natural science—is that the understanding of scripture and the interpretation of texts become, supposedly, superfluous, because first practical reason (see the "Philosophical Principles of the Interpretation of Scripture, for the Settlement of the Conflict" between the philosophical and the theological faculties, in I. Kant, *Der Streit der Fakultäten* (1798), Akademie ed., vol. 8, pp. 38ff.) and then exact nature finally no longer explain scripture and texts, but rather replace them: the sanification of hermeneutics, begun in Spinoza's manner, finally—following the logic of its later path into exactitude—sanifies it out of existence.

36. The opening up, in this connection, of the range of what is worthy of interpreta-

tion by hermeneutics is strikingly documented by the texts assembled by H.-G. Gadamer and G. Boehm in *Seminar: Philosophische Hermeneutik* (Frankfurt, 1976): at first what is interesting for hermeneutics—from Flavius through Rambach to S. J. Baumgarten—is only, or primarily, the Bible, then also the classical poets (F. A. Wolf) and classical philosophers (F. Ast), then—in a direction suggested by the dialogue—the whole of literature, in other words, all texts (this position being represented by Schleiermacher, who even poses the question "whether such authors as those who write for newspapers and those who draw up the various advertisements in them are subjects for the art of interpretation" [p. 136]), then all "expressions of life" (Dilthey) and there, in exemplary fashion, that of the "care"-world of what is "ready to hand" (Heidegger), and finally everything linguistic (Gadamer). This process of the increasing "universality" of hermeneutics should not be understood by means of the concept of linear progress that the hermeneuticists elsewhere attack, but in a different way, as the attempt to disarm the absolute text, the Bible—which is so explosive as to endanger life—by incorporating it, through assimilation, into a circle of interpretanda that is drawn more and more widely, making the Bible a relative text. It should be understood as a reply to the trauma—reactualized by the French Revolution—of hermeneutic civil war over the absolute text.

37. On the distinction between "discourses" and "endless discussions," see my contribution to W. Oelmüller, ed., *Normenbegründung—Normendurchsetzung* (Paderborn: Schöningh, 1978), pp. 230ff.

38. See W. Dilthey, *Der Aufbau der geschichtlichen Welt in den Geisteswissenschaften* (1910), in *Gesammelte Schriften* (6th ed., Göttingen/Stuttgart, 1973), vol. 7, p. 217: "The skillful comprehension of expressions of life which are fixed in lasting form we call 'interpretation.'. . . And the science of this art is hermeneutics"; as well as p. 131: "The essence of what dawns on us in experiencing and understanding is life."

39. H.-G. Gadamer, *Wahrheit und Methode,* esp. pp. 97ff., or *Truth and Method,* 90ff. I understand this as a corrective against Heidegger's re-"commitment" (*engagement*) of hermeneutics by tying it into everyday/practical "care" and existentiell/existential "resoluteness," by which Heidegger risks the loss of its capacity for neutralization and of its potential for distancing and unburdening, so that it is precisely with Heidegger—contrary to his fundamental position— that the ideological hermeneutics can link up.

40. Part of this can be the salutary superficialization of questions of truth and salvation. That can include the position of irony in the sense proposed by Thomas Mann, "Ironie und Radikalismus," in *Betrachtungen eines Unpolitischen* (1918; Frankfurt, 1956), p. 560: " '*Fiat justitia or libertas, fiat spiritus—pereat mundus et vita!*' Thus speaks all radicalism. 'Is the truth an argument—when it is a question of life?' This is the formula of irony." It is, it seems to me, the formula of literary hermeneutics, the formula by which it

directs us to esthetic matters. That touches on the problem of "application." One of the most important things, in connection with application, can be not to let it happen immediately. Where, for example, application, as judgment, means condemnation, it can be vitally important to delay it: to make it dilatory, of little or even of no effect. That is the basic character of esthetic application: as a reply to the civil war over the absolute text, hermeneutics neutralizes absolute texts, turning them into interpretable ones—into texts that can always be read in a different way and can always mean something different, and are therefore open to interpretation—and neutralizes absolute readers, turning them into esthetic ones.

41. Even H.-G. Gadamer calls, in connection with it, for a "rediscovery of the fundamental hermeneutic problem" (*Wahrheit und Methode,* pp. 290ff., or *Truth and Method,* pp. 274ff.) through an effort to "redefine the hermeneutics of the cultural sciences in terms of legal and theological hermeneutics" (*Wahrheit und Methode,* p. 294, or *Truth and Method,* p. 277); but, however fruitful this may be in a moderate form, in a case of excess it could lead again to a situation in which, with the return to a potentially deadly dogmatism of truth as a result of taking our orientation from the "dogmatic" faculties, the question of how we can live with the truth again becomes unanswerable. Of course that is something that does not so much need to be asserted in relation to Gadamer, but far more in relation, for example, to J. Habermas, "Der Universalitätsanspruch der Hermeneutik," in R. Bubner, K. Cramer, and R. Wiehl, eds., *Hermeneutik und Dialektik* (Tübingen, 1970), pp. 73–103.

42. L. Geldsetzer, "Traditionelle Institutionen philosophischer Lehre und Forschung," in H. M. Baumgartner, O. Höffe, and C. Wild, eds., *Philosophie—Gesellschaft—Planung, Colloquium, H. Krings zum Geburtstag* (2nd ed.; Munich, 1976), esp. p. 32.

43. K. Löwith, *Meaning in History* (Chicago, 1949), or *Weltgeschichte und Heilsgeschehen* (Stuttgart, 1953).

44. R. Koselleck, *Vergangene Zukunft* (cited in n. 22), esp. pp. 47ff.

45. Compare the analysis of the fundamental pattern in R. Koselleck, *Kritik und Krise. Ein Beitrag zur Pathogenese der bürgerlichen Welt* (1959; 2nd ed.; Freiburg/Munich, 1969), esp. pp. 7ff. and 155–57.

46. Compare my "In Praise of Polytheism. About Monomythic and Polymythic Thinking," in this volume.

47. Compare J. G. Fichte, *System der Sittenlehre nach den Prinzipien der Wissenschaft* (1798), sec. 31.

48. *Competentia* was the status of the *competentes:* in ancient Rome, of the candidates for the office of consul, later of candidates to be the pope and of other aspirants (for example to baptism), as long as they were not yet (or in the end did not become) what they were candidates for. "Competent . . . is the term for one who, together with others, sues for something": J. H. Zedler, *Grosses*

vollständiges Universallexikon aller Wissenschaften und Künste (Halle/Leipzig, 1732 and subsequent eds.).

49. T. W. Adorno, "Gesellschaft," in H. Kunst and S. Grundmann, eds., *Evangelisches Staatslexikon* (Stuttgart/Berlin, 1966), pp. 636–42, esp. p. 638.

50. W. Dilthey, *Gesammelte Schriften* (cited in n. 38), vol. 7, p. 225: "Interpretation would be impossible if expressions of life were entirely foreign. It would be unnecessary if there was nothing foreign in them. So it lies between these two extreme poles." This is the source of the inevitability of the so-called circle in understanding or hermeneutic circle: see M. Heidegger, *Sein und Zeit*, esp. pp. 152ff., or *Being and Time*, pp. 193ff., and H.-G. Gadamer, *Wahrheit und Methode*, esp. pp. 250ff., or *Truth and Method*, pp. 235ff. On the early history of this "task circle," see F. Rodi, " 'Erkenntnis des Erkannten'—August Boeckhs Grundformel der hermeneutischen Wissenschaften," in H. Flashar, K. Gründer, and A. Horstmann, eds., *Philologie und Hermeneutik im 19. Jahrhundert* (Göttingen, 1979), pp. 68–83. Heidegger's principle always holds (*Sein und Zeit*, p. 153; *Being and Time*, p. 195), that "What is decisive is not to get out of the circle but to come into it the right way."

51. For example: O. Brunner, W. Conze, and R. Koselleck, eds., *Geschichtliche Grundbegriffe. Historisches Lexikon zur politisch-sozialen Sprache in Deutschland* (Stuttgart; Klett, 1972); J. Ritter and K. Gründer, eds., *Historisches Wörterbuch der Philosophie* (Basel/Stuttgart: Schwabe, 1971); E. Rothacker and (subsequently) K. Gründer, eds., *Archiv für Begriffsgeschichte* (beginning in 1955).

Translator's Notes

a. "Lesen und Lesenlassen!"—a pun on "Leben und Lebenlassen!," "Live and let live."

b. "*Naherwartung*," the term used for the vivid expectation of the impending end of the world or Second Coming of Christ.

c. Compare the eleventh of Marx's theses on Feuerbach: "The philosophers have only *interpreted* the world in various ways; the point is to *change* it."

d. "*Eigentlich*": really, authentically, properly; Heidegger's term.

e. "*Antiprinzipielles Prinzip*": suggesting that this law of inertia is not a "matter of principle," as intentional changes might be.

f. A variant of the much-quoted Hobbesian principle, *Auctoritas, non veritas, facit legem* (authority, not truth, makes something a law).

g. In German, "story" and "history" are one word, *Geschichte*, so the transition from stories (*Geschichten*) to history (*die Geschichte*) requires only the addition of the definite article.

h. "Divide and drive away!"—a variant of the famous *Divide et impera*: "Divide and rule."

i. This sentence is in English in the original.

Note on the Texts Collected in This Volume

"Farewell to Matters of Principle (Another Autobiographical Introduction)" was first published (as "Abschied vom Prinzipiellen. Auch eine autobiographische Einleitung") in 1981 in *Abschied vom Principiellen* (Stuttgart: Philipp Reclam jun.).

"Competence in Compensating for Incompetence? (On the Competence and Incompetence of Philosophy)" was a lecture given in Munich, September 28, 1973. It was first published in Hans M. Baumgartner, Otfried Höffe, and Christoph Wild, eds., *Philosophie—Gesellschaft—Planung. Kolloquium, Hermann Krings zum 60. Geburtstag* (Munich: Bayerisches Staatsinstitut für Hochschulforschung und Hochschulplanung, 1974), pp. 114–25, and reprinted in *Philosophisches Jahrbuch 81* (1974), pp. 341–49, and *Giessener Universitätsblätter*, 1 (1974), pp. 89–99.

"Indicted and Unburdened Man in Eighteenth-Century Philosophy" was a lecture given at the Herzog-August-Bibliothek in Wolfenbüttel, November 23, 1978. It was first published in Bernhard Fabian, Wilhelm Schmidt-Biggemann, and Rudolf Vierhaus, eds., *Deutschlands kulturelle Entfaltung: die Neubestimmung des Menschen* (Munich: Kraus, 1980), pp. 193–209.

"The End of Fate? (Some Remarks on the Inevitability of Things Over Which We Have No Disposition)" was a lecture given at the Carl Friedrich von Siemens Foundation in Munich, June 21, 1976, and first published in *Schicksal? Grenzen der Machbarkeit. Ein Symposion. Mit einem Nachwort von Mohammed Rassem* (Munich: Deutscher Taschenbuch Verlag, 1977), pp. 7–25.

"In Praise of Polytheism (On Monomythical and Polymythical Thinking)" was a lecture given at the Technical University in Berlin, January 31, 1978, and first published in Hans Poser, ed., *Philosophie und Mythos. Ein Kolloquium* (Berlin/ New York: de Gruyter, 1979), pp. 40–58.

"The Question, To What Question Is Hermeneutics the Answer?" was a lecture given at the University in Tübingen, November 26, 1979, and published in *Philosophisches Jahrbuch*, 88 (1981), pp. 1–19.

Books by Odo Marquard

Skeptische Methode im Blick auf Kant (Freiburg/Munich: Alber, 1958; 3rd printing, 1982).

Schwierigkeiten mit der Geschichtsphilosophie (Frankfurt: Suhrkamp, 1973; 2nd ed., 1982: suhrkamp taschenbuch wissenschaft no. 394).

Abschied vom Prinzipiellen. Philosophische Studien. Reclams Universal-Bibliothek no. 7724 [2] (Stuttgaart: Reclam, 1981).

Krise der Erwartung—Stunde der Erfahrung. Zur ästhetischen Kompensation des modernen Erfahrungsverlustes (Konstanz: Konstanzer Universitätsverlag, 1982).

Transzendentaler Idealismus, romantische Naturphilosophie, Psychoanalyse (Cologne: Dinter, 1987).

Apologie des Zufälligen. Philosophische Studien, Reclams Universal-Bibliothek no. 8351 [2] (Stuttgart: Reclam, 1986).

Ästhetica und Anästhetica. Zur Philosophie der schönen und nicht mehr schönen Kunst (Paderborn: Schöningh, 1987).

Name Index

Adorno, T., 8, 35, 88, 126, 128
Andersen, H. C., 91
Aristotle, 3, 89, 101, 121
Augustine, 48, 50
Azaïs, P.-H., 43

Bachofen, J. J., 99
Baeumler, A., 103
Barthes, R., 103
Baumgarten, A. G., 40
Bayle, P., 4, 43
Benn, G., 91
Bentham, J., 44
Blumenberg, H., 17, 74, 89, 91, 112
Bohr, N., 25, 36 n
Bougainville, L. A. de, 51
Brecht, B., 10–11
Büchner, G., 79
Bultmann, 88
Burckhardt, J., 4, 43
Burke, E., 40

Charron, 4
Chastellux, Chevalier de, 44
Chomsky, N., 23
Cicero, 42
Collingwood, R. G., 112–13
Comte, A., 88
Cournot, A., 43
Creuzer, F., 99–100

Dannhauer, J. C., 121
Descartes, R., 40, 45, 121
Dilthey, W., 124, 135 n
Durkheim, E., 128

Emerson, R. W., 43

Fichte, J. G., 39, 54, 66, 71, 76
Forster, G., 51
Freud, S., 8–9, 31, 35, 67
Frisch, M., 91
Fuhrmann, M., 48

Gadamer, H.-G., 112–13, 124, 135 n
Gehlen, A., 29, 37, 89
Geldsetzer, L., 125
Gide, A., 12
Goethe, 9, 67, 99
Görres, 99
Grillparzer, F., 67

Habermas, J., 23, 70
Hegel, G. W. F., 70, 100
Heidegger, M., 27, 35, 70–71, 88, 115,
  135 n
Heine, H., 8
Helvetius, C. A., 44
Herder, J. G., 40, 44
Heyne, C. G., 51, 98–99
Hölderlin, F., 67, 71
Horkheimer, M., 8, 88
Humboldt, W. v., 40
Hume, D., 4, 47

Jauss, H. R., 11, 112, 124
Jung, C. G., 67
Justin, 84 n

Kant, I., 7, 34, 40, 42–44, 48, 54, 56,
  71, 76

141

Subject Index

anthropology, 40, 53; after end of humanity, 79; medical, 52; philosophical, 40–41, 45–46, 50, 52, 61 n, 73

art: becoming esthetic of, 53; fate as category of, 67; as holiday from tribunal, 53; symbolic and abstract in Hegel, 100. *See also* esthetics; literary

asceticism, 9; and totemism, 9

atheism, 47, 70–71; antitheological, 71; theological, 70–71. *See also* disenchantment; God

beginning, 73–74, 77, 82; absolute, 73–74, 77. *See also* change; derivativeness; pregiven

being: history of, 70; as pseudonym for God, 70; withdrawal of, 70–71, 85 n

"bonum-through-malum" idea, 44–45, 49

change, 77, 116–19, 125; burden of proof on one who proposes, 14, 16, 74, 117; dominated by derivation, 117; and philosophy of principles, 16; total, 15, 116, 118. *See also* transitoriness

choice. *See* nonchoice

Christianity, 48, 95–98, 107 n, 121, 125; antifatalism of, 68–69

code, 127–29. *See also* hermeneutics; linguistics

community, 77

compensation, 42–45, 79–81; for loss of life-world, 41; mechanism of, 43; for overtribunalization, 41; for philosophy's reduction in competence, 23, 28, 34; as program of social reform, 43–44; revolt as, 10

competence, 6; in compensating for incompetence, 28, 34, 87; definition of, 136 n; nostalgia for, 28–30; of philosophy, 22–36, 87. *See also* incompetence

conscience: as absolute principle, 15; bad, 55; having vs. being, 11, 30–33, 38, 55–56; of philosophy, 30–31; of postwar Germany, 10; more solitary than universal, 16

consensus, 124

consequences: lack of disposition over, 17, 64, 76–81

conservatism, 15; is unavoidable, 74

contingency, 16–18; of philosophy, 105

Critical Theory, 8, 11, 70

critique, 11, 31–32; of alienation, 11; global, 117; of ideology, 13, 56, 93, 117; of metaphysics, 73; of myths, 88–93; as unburdening, 31–32. *See also* philosophy, critical